MW01108987

Psychology through Literature

Patrick White, Ed.D.

Cover Art by Heather Bellgardt

DEDICATED TO DR. RALPH WHITE

A teacher to the teachers

ACKNOWLEDGEMENTS

This book would not have been possible without the many students throughout the years in my English and Psychology classes. Our class discussions produced much of the insight you will find here. To all of you, I am deeply thankful for your presence and contributions.

I'd also like to thank Dr. Jean Kleine-Kracht, who gave up time during her summer vacation to provide valuable editorial insights.

Most of all, I'd like to thank my wife, Catherine White. It's not easy being the spouse of an English teacher! Her patience, kindness, and support mean everything, and I am deeply grateful.

CONTENTS

INTRODUCTION

In the spring of 2006, our social studies department chair, Mrs. Best, asked me whether I knew any teacher with a psychology certification. It seemed odd that she would ask me since I was in the English Department. But nonetheless, she asked. I told her that yes, I knew someone (myself), but I had no desire to teach psychology. I was thoroughly comfortable teaching AP Language and Composition and didn't want the extra teaching load.

Over the weekend, that "still small voice" urged me to think again. Teaching psychology would grant much more freedom than English since it wasn't associated with state testing. In other words, I had the promise of more autonomy in teaching my classes.

On Monday I went back to Mrs. Best and agreed to teach the class. With no materials and no experience with the course, I harbored some fear and trepidation. But by the fall,

I was moving forward, and my students and I had wonderful, engaging discussions as we shared our life experiences in connection to various psychological theories. The class was much more interesting, engaging, and personable than any other class I taught.

Then something unexpected happened.

The discussions in my English classes were also enriched. Nearly every short story, novel, and poem we read had a connection to psychology. It was in the merging of these two fields that I discovered this principle:

Psychology is the <u>study</u> of human behavior. Literature includes the <u>stories</u> of human behavior.

Strip away the top layers of literature, and you'll find psychology. I was absolutely amazed at the geyser I had struck! Reading literature would never be the same for me. The merging of these two worlds has been wonderful, thought-provoking, and inspiring for me.

Now--over a decade later--I'd like to share from a literary perspective how the lives of fictional characters can lead us to a deeper and more meaningful appreciation for psychological theory. If you already have a background in psychology, this book may offer you literary insight. If you've never taken a course in psychology, this book will offer some of the basic theories often found in introductory psychology courses.

I hope you find the journey as enlightening and inspiring as I have.

Patrick White / July 2019

CHAPTER ONE

TENSION OF OPPOSITES

We all have problems, right? You can't be human and escape those. It starts from the moment you hear the alarm starting another school day, and all you want to do is *sleep*! Or you're sitting in class completely and woefully unprepared for that multiple-choice test on *The Great Gatsby*. Or you just got a text from your mom telling you to pick up your sister after school, and you're wondering, "What—again? Are you serious?"

Believe it or not, all these have something in common at their very core: the *tension of opposites*. Morrie Schwartz describes it best: "Have I told you about the tension of opposites?...Life is a series of pulls back and forth. You want to do one thing, but you are bound to do something else."

In other words, no matter what the problem in life (or literature), you can always, *always* find some opposing forces that are diametrically opposed to each other. The Irish novelist Laurence Stern says it this way:

"No body, but he who has felt it, can conceive what a plaguing thing it is to have a man's mind torn asunder by two projects of equal strength, both obstinately pulling in a contrary direction at the same time."

Why is this? Because we human beings are conflicted creatures. No matter your age, IQ, race, nationality, social status, education, etc., we *ALL* have conflicting impulses inside of us. This is true in life. And it's true in literature.

And why? (Notice I keep asking *why*. That's a tool you can always use to dig deeper into literature.)

Literature (at least the kind studied in English classes), can simply be a mirror for the natural world--the world we human beings actually live and breathe in. Fictional characters in literature are alive. They are imbued with the spirit of life given to them by their authors. Whatever we feel and experience, *they* feel and experience.

So we're all stuck with our tension of opposites.

Go ahead...check it out right now. Chances are you have some tension of opposites lurking inside of you

15

wherever you're sitting. Maybe you feel the need to read this book right now, but that is being contrasted by your desire to go to the kitchen and eat that bag of Nacho Cheese Doritos.

Or check your phone.

Or take a nap.

Or pretty much anything else under the sun. (Hey, it's okay...it won't hurt my feelings.)

Whatever it is, we could clarify that conflict as *need vs. desire.*

Let's go deeper.

Maybe your best friend stopped talking to you last semester-- and you have absolutely no idea why. Maybe that friendship ended with no resolution and no communication. Maybe more than anything in the world, you want to talk to her and find out why she stopped being your friend.

But you don't dare. Just the mere thought of it makes you nervous and anxious. Deep down in there is a love-hate relationship. *Love vs. fear.*

Tension of opposites.

We could do this all day, but the point is that the human mind is always in a tug of war somewhere, somehow.

Literature has faithfully chronicled, explored, and plumbed this pattern throughout human history. And identifying this pattern becomes a valuable tool in our quest for digging into the human psyche in literature and in life.

Finding opposing forces is a great starting point when examining any moment in literature. And I mean *any* moment. It could be something big, like the Battle of Five Armies in *The Hobbit*.

Or something small, like a simile in *Peter Pan* (for example: "Her romantic mind was like tiny boxes, one within the other, that come from the puzzling East...").

If you're going to be a human being, or a character in literature, you just can't escape the tug-of-war within the human psyche. And by analyzing the tension of opposites in the lives of literary characters, we can learn about our own struggles within.

Now let's take out our pipe and notepad, sit in our big comfy chair, and listen as our literary characters lie on the couch and tell us their problems, one at a time...

"And how do you *feel* about that?"

CHAPTER TWO

WHICH OPPOSITES?

We've all been in love, right? Well, maybe not. But we've all at least thought we were. Maybe it was that paragon of perfection who sat right in front of you in English class--the one who turned you into a useless, excited lump of goo every time she glanced back in your direction. And then you realized she was just looking at the clock to see how much time was left in class. (...*Sigh*!)

Maybe that's why we often start our literary journey in high school with *Romeo and Juliet*. Let's use the opposing forces theory on these two star-crossed lovers. When Juliet delivers that famous balcony soliloquy, she walks right into the crosshairs of a psychological tug of war.

What are they? On one side, is her incredible **desire for Romeo**. On the other side is **duty to her family**.

If you are writing an essay on this topic, you want to be as precise as possible. You could describe these opposing forces with a few phrases, but it's more precise to use nouns to depict each force. We could then say *the **balcony scene dramatizes Juliet's psychological forces of love vs. duty***. If you state that in your introduction, you immediately show your teacher that you are digging beneath the surface. In other words, you're using psychological analysis.

You might be thinking, "What do I do from there? It's great to have a thesis statement, but what about the rest of the essay?"

Patience, Young Grasshopper. First, you learn kung-fu grip. Then you learn to fight. In other words, that comes later. For now, let's practice finding opposing psychological forces in other novels and plays.

Of Mice and Men has one of the most gut-wrenching endings of any novel. (*Spoiler alert!* If you haven't read it...look away!)

George is squatting behind an unsuspecting Lenny, quietly holding a gun to his head. A mob of blood-thirsty men, led by that no-good weasel Curly, are closing in. If George does nothing, they'll give Lenny a painful and merciless death. However, Lenny could die quickly and painlessly if George simply pulls the trigger.

Poor George is caught between two terrible psychological forces. What are they? We could say **love for his friend vs. fear of responsibility**. That is, being the one responsible for his death. And he must make the decision lightning quick. No time to analyze. Wow.

This is a common technique that writers use. I call it the "boiling water metaphor." Writers invariably put their characters in a pot of water and then turn up the heat. **Once applied, the heat brings opposing psychological forces. How they respond defines their character. You can find this strategy in virtually every novel.**

Why is it so common? Again, literature is a mirror for life. This same metaphor applies to us in our own lives. We live with opposing forces. **How we respond defines who we are.**

In *The Odyssey*, Odysseus is hit with some formidable opposing forces. All he wants to do is return home to his wife Penelope, but unfortunately, he's surrounded by a crew of idiots, angry gods, and monsters. (Sounds like a typical high school to me. But I digress.)

Despite this hostile external environment, the real struggle lies within. Inside his own mind.

When he passes by the Island of the Sirens, he knows that no man can resist the enticing song of its beautiful inhabitants. No man has conquered this temptation. What man can resist?

Evidently, not even Odysseus with all his strength of will. He just *has* to hear that song! But he knows that it will weaken him at the knees, and he will order the ship towards the shore, only to break apart on the deadly rocks.

What psychological forces are acting upon him? This is **temptation vs. impulse control**. Or **sexual drive vs. fidelity**. Or **curiosity vs. survival**. Take your pick...or come up with your own variations. The idea is to pinpoint specific nouns that fight over a character's psychological well being.

On that note, impulse control shows up in many, many psychological conflicts. Characters must often make their choices lightning fast as the water boils around them--so they often don't have time to deliberate. Often, they make their choices impulsively, which reveals this psychological axiom:

Impulse control is the most fundamental psychological skill. Master it, and you thrive. Lose it, and you suffer.

Just ask Hamlet. This literary rock star has been accused of thinking too much and for too long. Many critics argue he should have taken action immediately and killed Claudius for the murder of his father. But his impulsive killing of Polonius sets off a chain of events, leading to the deaths of Ophelia, Laertes, Gertrude, Claudius, and Hamlet himself. The moment he drives the sword through the curtain into Polonius's belly is the result of opposing forces: **rage vs. impulse control**. In this case, it is rage towards his mother for marrying Claudius. He demonstrates impulse control through much of the play, but the one moment he loses that battle, he unleashes the specter of death.

John Proctor in *The Crucible* is also a man tormented with opposing forces. Okay, so the man cheated on his wife with Abigail Williams--a girl half his age, no less.

What do we have here: **morality vs. lust**? Sure, but that's just the start for poor Proctor. Once he failed that test, he is overcome with guilt and remorse.

In the courtroom, when Abigail pretends to be possessed by Mary Warren, Proctor loses it. He grabs Abigail by the hair, calls her a few choice names, and confesses his affair to Judge Danforth. Opposing forces for Proctor in this moment? **Self-loathing vs. Truth. Self-preservation vs. Justice. Rage vs. Impulse control**. (Sound familiar?) Also notice that he later signs the witchcraft confession, rips it up in a fit of anger, and then chooses to go to the gallows. He decides to die for his honor in a moment's decision. He is a man of impulsivity.

Pride and Prejudice is a crowd favorite (at least with the ladies). Elizabeth Bennet has a psychological moment of self-discovery when Darcy gives her the letter explaining his actions against Wickham. Upon realizing that she completely misjudged the poor bloke, she exclaims, "Till this moment I never knew myself!"

Are there opposing forces acting upon her? You better believe it. **Vanity vs. Humility**. **Judgment vs. Acceptance**. **Ignorance vs. Knowledge**. The list goes on.

We could keep going with the entire canon of literature, but by now you see that opposing psychological forces are inherent with nearly all characters.

Now a word about these forces...

Force #1 is usually pretty obvious. In other words, most readers can easily see this force acting upon the character. But Force #2 is usually more obscure. It's usually hidden beneath the surface. The way to find it is to think of the **emotional *opposite*** of Force #1.

For example, *The Scarlet Letter*'s Hester Prynne is under pressure to reveal the name of the father of her illegitimate child. Most readers can easily identify this pressure as Force #1. But what is Force #2? It's opposite. Why does she not want to confess? Because she doesn't want to incriminate the man she loves, Arthur Dimmesdale. Force #1 is obvious to everyone--at least to the crowd of Puritans who are jeering at Hester on the scaffold. But Force #2 lies unseen to the naked eye. Hester is stricken with the opposing forces of

25

coercion vs. love. One is observable while the other is hidden.

The chart below shows different types of opposing forces. All the terms in the left column are varieties of Force #1, which is more external. The terms in the right column represent the deeper, more hidden forces. You could probably think of others on your own, which would expand your emotional vocabulary.

Force #1	vs.	Force #2
Explicit	vs.	Implicit
External	vs.	Internal
Observable	vs.	Hidden
Physical	vs.	Non-physical
Behavior	vs.	Need
Seen	vs.	Invisible
Body	vs.	Spirit
Desire	vs.	Need
Corporeal	vs.	Essence

Now, back to you.

You may be under opposing forces as we speak. Although you're reading this book, you'd really prefer to eat a bag of Doritos and surf your phone. We'll call that Force #1. It's easy to see or feel it. It's loud and clear. It's *explicit*.

Force #2 is a little buried. *Why* are you resisting the impulse to stop reading and do whatever you want? Maybe you have a desire to improve your essay skills.

Aha! This is Force #2. So this moment in your life depicts the **clash between the explicit forces of the munchies and phone addiction against the implicit force for intellectual growth.**

Using precise terms like these to nail down your psychological analysis of literature is guaranteed to impress your English teacher. And that's what it's all about, right?

But as the proctologist said as he snapped on his plastic gloves, "Let's go deeper, shall we?"

Those opposing forces don't exist in a vacuum. In other words, they didn't just fall out of the sky. There are other forces around them, too. Here's a basic mock up of the process:

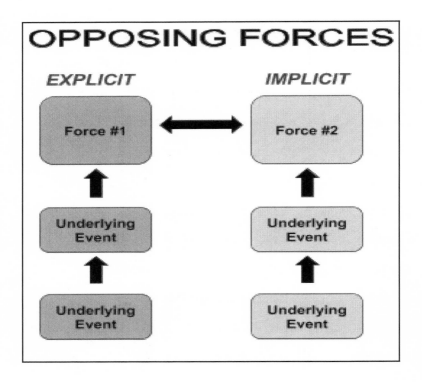

Here's how it works:

Each opposing force has a preceding, underlying event that brings it into existence. That event, in turn, has a preceding event that caused *it* to occur. It's like the game of dominoes: each domino falls on the one next to it, which causes the next to one fall, and so on.

This chart is only a snapshot of the process. You can trace events back and back (or forward and forward).

Everything is linked to something else. Our information is always limited or incomplete--that's why no literary analyses are absolute and final. *There's always more to the story than any one person knows*. As Confucius said, "When you do not know a thing, to allow that you do not know it; this is knowledge."

But enough ancient Chinese wisdom...we need an example.

Being one of the most recognizable and well known literary characters, Hamlet will do just fine. We already identified one of his conflicts and *rage vs. impulse control*, but more digging may look like this:

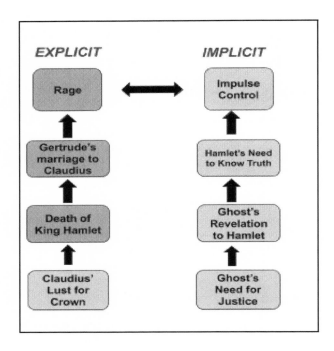

EXPLICIT

Rage ⟷ Impulse Control

Gertrude's marriage to Claudius → Hamlet's Need to Know Truth

Death of King Hamlet → Ghost's Revelation to Hamlet

Claudius' Lust for Crown → Ghost's Need for Justice

IMPLICIT

Let's use that infamous moment when Hamlet kills Polonius:

Queen: What will thou do? thou will not murder me?
Help, ho!

Polonius [behind the arras]: What, ho! Help!

Hamlet: How now, a rat? Dead for a ducat, dead. [He kills Polonius by thrusting a rapier through the arras.]

Polonius [behind the arras]: Oh, I am slain!

Queen: Oh, me! What has thou done?

Hamlet: Nay, I know not.

Short and sweet, huh? Ah, deceptively so.

Hamlet is caught in a torrent of psychological forces here, and his assessment is "I don't know." His psychological self-awareness might be MIA, but that's where we come in. Let's get him on the psychological couch...

In the moment when Hamlet heard a noise behind the arras (curtain), he probably thought Claudius was hiding behind there. After all, he's married to Hamlet's mother Gertrude, and they are standing in the royal bedroom. On the surface, Hamlet's conflict is *rage vs. impulse control.* His rage that drives his sword through the curtain is caused by his *mother's marrying Claudius.* This rage is the most obvious (explicit) force acting on him in this moment.

But what caused her to marry the murderous Claudius? The *death of her husband, King Hamlet.* But don't stop there. What caused his death? *Claudius' lust for power* led him to murder his brother, steal the crown, and take his wife. So like a stream of dominoes, the events line up and fall upon Hamlet's frail, grief-stricken psyche.

But hey, that's only half the picture! We have the *implicit* force on the other side of Hamlet. Opposing his rage is his need for *impulse control.* He needs to save his vengeance for the right person at the right time. He hasn't yet killed Claudius because he needed to *confirm the honesty of the ghost's version.* And why does he need to do that? Because the ghost told him the secret of death: he was murdered in his sleep by his brother Claudius. And why did the Ghost tell this story to Hamlet? *Because he wants justice for his spilled blood.*

(Actually, there was no blood. It was poison, but you get the point.)

Notice that all the events on the left side of the chart are negative events. Unpleasant, to say the least. And all the events on the right side tend to be positive. That may not always be the case, but it's an interesting pattern.

Also, in this critical moment--this crucible of events for Hamlet--he fails to exert impulse control against his rage. Without hesitation, he plunges his sword into the curtain, killing the well-intentioned, bumbling Polonius. But as I said before, this is only a snapshot. There are more dominoes that fall as a result of this conflict. You can chart each one beginning with the opposing forces and go from there.

Practice this method as you read literature, and you will get better and better at finding psychological depth to your characters. And while you're at it, you might want to apply the process to your own actions as well. And when you do, you may realize that literature has a great deal to reveal about yourself.

After all, a little growth never hurt anybody, right?

CHAPTER THREE

IT'S ALL ABOUT NEEDS

Once you've mastered the opposing forces game, it's time to move on to further diagnosis. In other words, you have a working thesis, and now you need to elaborate on those body paragraphs.

Again, this is where psychology comes to the rescue.

One of the main purposes of psychology is to figure out *why people do what they do* (i.e., to explain human behavior). If we live in a cause-and-effect universe, there is *always* a reason something happens. In other words, people don't do things without a reason or stimulus. (Sometimes, they do things for no *good* reason, but that's a discussion for another day.)

Human behavior doesn't exist in a vacuum. It's like the dominoes that fall on each other in succession. One falls on the other...which falls on the other...which falls on the other, etc.

Psychological theories are helpful in identifying the preceding domino, but remember you can *always* find exceptions. That's because human behavior is very complex and difficult to predict. However, one nearly universal idea is **drive-reduction theory**, which posits that we are *always* in a state of need. (Think about it…you have multiple needs assailing you at this very moment!) As a result of this need, we strive for homeostasis (or state of balance). Drive-reduction theory states that when a physiological need arises, a psychological drive kicks in to motivate us to satisfy it.

Let's find a literary example. In *Their Eyes Were Watching God*, Janie first meets her husband Joe Starks on a dirt road while tending the farm. Joe is on his way to Eatonville to become the first mayor of a town governed by African-Americans:

[Joe] had always wanted to be a big voice, but da white folks had all de sayso where he come from and everywhere else, exceptin' dis place dat colored folks was building theirselves….De man dat built things oughta boss it….He

36

meant to git dere whilst de town wuz yet a baby. He meant to

buy in big. It had always been his wish and desire to be a

big voice and he had to live nearly thirty years to find a

chance.

What is Joe's need? As a black man in the Jim Crow

South, Joe has been subjugated by white society. No doubt

they have denied him resources--material and psychological.

This denial of sustenance also affects his self-esteem. He

yearns for acknowledgement and validation. This void

creates a hole in his psyche--one that can only be filled with

the admiration of others. To fill this hole, he must become the

mayor of Eatonville and prove to others (and himself) that he

is worthy.

Joe's drive can only be satisfied with political power. He

seeks to find psychological homeostasis by placing himself in

a position above others. Sadly, this includes his wife as he

stomps all over Janie's emotional needs in an attempt to

satisfy his own.

You can find a drive, a need, with all characters in

literature. Drive-reduction theory explains virtually *any*

37

conflict, but identifying the need is just the beginning. We

need more.

Let's check out Abraham Maslow's **Hierarchy of Needs**.

This theory identifies specific types of needs and the order in

which we seek to satisfy them. And It all starts with the

pyramid....

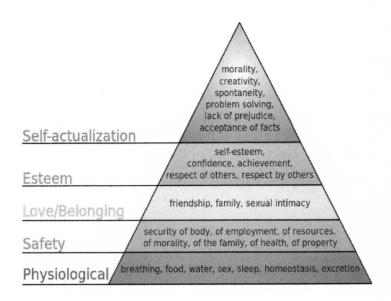

MASLOW'S HIERARCHY OF NEEDS

Self-actualization — morality, creativity, spontaneity, problem solving, lack of prejudice, acceptance of facts

Esteem — self-esteem, confidence, achievement, respect of others, respect by others

Love/Belonging — friendship, family, sexual intimacy

Safety — security of body, of employment, of resources, of morality, of the family, of health, of property

Physiological — breathing, food, water, sex, sleep, homeostasis, excretion

Maslow theorized that lower level needs outweigh higher

level needs. In other words, your physiological needs are the most important. Then safety needs. Then love and belonging needs, etc. For example, if you have to go the bathroom in class, it's really hard to pay attention to the class discussion. When you gotta go, you gotta go--right?

Or if someone has a chokehold on you, and you can't breathe, you're not too worried about world peace at that moment.

Maslow has his critics. They argue that many people are willing to die for a moral belief (soldiers, martyrs, mothers with children in a burning building, etc.). These folks would have a different order of human needs. But the bottom line is **we all have essentially the same human needs**, and once you identify those needs in the lives of literary characters, you have hit a geyser for literary analysis and discussion.

Now, let's play literary psychologist...shall we?

According to Maslow, human beings seek first to satisfy their physiological needs. These include breathing, food, water, sex, sleep, homeostasis, and excretion. You could probably think of a few others that aren't listed there, but you get the picture. We have an instinctive need for physical survival, and if events threaten these needs, nothing else matters.

At the beginning of *Night*, Elie Wiesel was so devout in his Jewish faith that prayer often caused him to weep. Before his family could flee, the Nazis forced them and their neighbors into cattle cars, where they were taken by train in horrid conditions to the death camps.

The journey through the night was long and brutal. Denied food, water, and sleep, the Jewish prisoners were packed like sardines into the train cars with unbearable heat. Suddenly, Madame Schachter began howling that she could see a furnace. The others saw nothing and concluded she had gone mad.

When she refused to stop, her fellow prisoners (who had been her neighbors) beat her over the head--right in front of her little boy, who just sat there quietly. At this point, most readers recoil in horror. What could cause people who had previously been normal, civilized, even friendly neighbors, to do something so brutal?

At the core of this is Maslow's theory that **human beings will do almost anything for survival**. If threatened under extreme circumstances, morality and social mores go out the window.

Since *Night* is non-fiction, does this apply to fictional characters, as well? Absolutely. Let's visit our favorite monster in *Frankenstein*.

After Victor Frankenstein creates the monster and immediately abandons him, the monster must forage for his own survival. First, he finds berries in the wilderness and then food left behind by campers:

It was morning when I awoke, and my first care was to visit the fire. I uncovered it, and a gentle breeze quickly fanned it into a flame....When night came again, I found, with pleasure, that the fire gave light as well as heat; and that the discovery of this element was useful to me in my food; for I had found some of the offals that the travellers had left had been roasted, and tasted much more savoury than the berries I had gathered from the trees. I tried, therefore, to dress my food in the same manner, placing it on the live embers. I found that the berries were spoiled by this operation, and the nuts and berries much improved.

Later, he takes clothes off a clothesline. He sleeps in an abandoned hut: *"I escaped to the open country, and fearfully took refuge in a low hovel, quite bare, and making a wretched appearance after the palaces I beheld in the village."* *The bottom line: he first directs his attention towards **physical survival**.*

After satisfying these bare necessities, he longs for human connection. His little hovel, or shed, is beside the house of the De Lacey family. As the monster spies on them, his need for love and belonging become evident:

[T]he old man…taking up an instrument, began to play, and to produce sounds sweeter than the voice of the thrush or the nightingale. It was a lovely sight, even to me, poor wretch! who had never beheld aught beautiful before. The silver hair and benevolent countenance of the aged cottager won my reverence, while the gentle manners of the girl enticed my love. I felt sensations of a peculiar nature and overpowering nature: they were a mixture of pain and pleasure, such as I had never before experienced, either from hunger or cold, warmth or food; and I withdrew from the window, unable to bear these emotions.

Here, the monster longs for **safety and love**. He finally reaches out to blind, old De Lacey, only to be attacked by his son Felix, who is frightened to death by the hideousness of the monster and attacks him with a broom.

What effect does this have on our hapless hero? All he wants is acceptance and love! But nooo...time and time again, he is rejected by human beings, and so he declares war on the human race--especially on his creator, Victor Frankenstein.

Let's review. *Frankenstein* becomes a classic example for Maslow's theory. The monster seeks to satisfy his physical needs, then safety, then love and belonging. But after being attacked (and even shot after rescuing a young, drowning girl), all bets are off. His **self-esteem** plummets, and by no means does he reach **self-actualization**.

In other words, he doesn't pass Go...he doesn't collect two hundred dollars. Poor sap.

The human need for connection, found in Maslow's Love and Belonging stage, is one of the most universal and powerful forces. Never underestimate its ability to drive human behavior. You will find this need to be one of the most significant and common needs driving storylines.

Check out some student essays on Frankenstein, found in the appendix in the back of the book.

For Edna Pontellier in *The Awakening*, her love for Robert drives her to commit suicide by swimming out to sea and letting the tide take her. Janie Starks in *Their Eyes Were Watching* God goes through three marriages in pursuit of authentic love.

Of course, these are examples of romantic love, but often the need for love and belonging is much deeper and wider than that. Holden Caulfield in *The Catcher in the Rye* feels an existential loneliness and yearns for connection. He has the opportunity to avail himself of a prostitute's services, but chooses instead just to talk to her. The kid just wants somebody to connect with.

To illustrate the power of this type of love and belonging, consider the theories of Carl Rogers, one of the most influential humanistic psychologists of the twentieth century.

He believed the ability of a therapist to connect with his patient is *the* most important factor that brings about healing. It's even more important than the therapist's expertise or experience. Rogers believed that healing can only occur when human connection takes place.

The literary student can draw upon Maslow and Rogers to understand and explain much of the behavior of literary characters. This dynamic is found in much of poetry as well as novels. For example, Walt Whitman paints this picture in his poem "A Noiseless, Patient Spider."

A noiseless patient spider,
I mark'd where on a little promontory it stood isolated,
Mark'd how to explore the vacant vast surrounding,
It launch'd forth filament, filament, filament, out of itself,
Ever unreeling them, ever tirelessly speeding them.

And you O my soul where you stand,
Surrounded, detached, in measureless oceans of space,

Ceaselessly musing, venturing, throwing, seeking the

spheres to connect them,

Till the bridge you will need be form'd, till the ductile

anchor hold,

Till the gossamer thread you fling catch somewhere, O

my soul.

Here, the spider is casting his web (the filament) into the wind, just hoping it will latch on to something. Humans do the same thing. Whether Maslow placed the love and belonging stage in the right order on the pyramid or not, he is correct that we human beings (and our literary counterparts) absolutely must connect to survive.

The Grapes of Wrath has one of the most controversial endings in American literature. Seeing an old man dying of starvation, Rose of Sharon pulls out her breast and lets him nurse. She then smiles "mysteriously." Why does she do this?

Her baby had just died at birth. She is caught between the opposing forces of grief and love. By saving the old man, she fulfills a love and belonging need, once again connected to the human race. This is a healing moment for a grieving mother.

Sometimes, a pursuit of love also feeds the need for self-esteem--Maslow's next stage on the pyramid. Consider Jay Gatsby's overwhelming love for Daisy. Readers often swoon over his devotion to this femme fatale. After all, the man bought a mansion across the bay from her house just to be close to her! And then threw extravagant parties just in hopes that she might wander in! Sound like love to you?

Maybe. But let's go deeper. Psychologically.

Gatsby grew up poor. In his eyes, he was a nobody. He had to reinvent himself into a new identity. So James Gatz became Jay Gatsby, tycoon extraordinaire. And there was "Daisy, gleaming like silver, safe and proud above the hot struggles of the poor."

She was wooed by multiple suitors. *Everyone* wanted Daisy. If poor James Gatz could just get this girl, he would be somebody. It wasn't really about her beauty. Or even her wealth. It wasn't real love. It was her *status*. Landing this white whale would secure Gatsby's self-esteem needs.

Thanks, Maslow.

Before we hit the top of the pyramid, let's talk about this fundamental point. Maslow was a humanistic psychologist. This means he believed that *life is ultimately about growth*. Yes, we are needy creatures, but the whole point in satisfying those needs is growth.

This idea fits in well with literature because **the whole point of a novel is the self-discovery, or growth, of your protagonist**. Granted, not all of them get there, but an astute reader will grow vicariously by learning from the character's mistakes. Therefore, self-discovery belongs to the reader more than the literary character. In other words, the character might fail, but he passes the baton to the reader. Once again, the bottom line is *growth*.

The top of Maslow's pyramid is **self-actualization**. After satisfying all the needs below that level, self-actualized folks look towards their fellow human beings and ask, "How can I help?" Their focus is on the needs of others, and they want to make a positive splash in the river of humanity.

Siddhartha is a perfect example. This guy was born in a well-to-do family but left it all to meditate in the woods and find spiritual perfection. He meditates and becomes one with all the little critters in nature. Not good enough, though. He fails to find nirvana.

No soup for you, Siddhartha!

Ah, but then he has a son. Actually, he has a son who drives him crazy. Basically, your typical kid who never listens to his father and runs around like a chicken with his head cut off. But despite all this frustration, Siddhartha learns to love his son more than himself.

Bingo! The missing puzzle piece.

Or missing "peace." (I crack myself up sometimes.)

So Siddhartha could meditate until the cows come home. Or become one with the cows. But until he loved someone more than himself, he could not self-actualize.

See? You serve a purpose after all--at least for your parents.

Okay, so you're not into eastern literature and philosophy. (Actually, *Siddhartha* was written by a German).

So you're not into German literature. What else ya got?

Lots of literary characters never reach self-actualization. None of the boys in *Lord of the Flies* reach that level. (Talk about running around like a chicken with your head cut off...that's pretty much all these boys do!)

Or poor Winston Smith in *1984*. This guy "loved Big Brother" after being tortured by the same. Where's his growth?

Or Tom Wingfield in *The Glass Menagerie.* He leaves his poor mother and helpless sister to fend for themselves while he goes off to play in the Merchant Marines. He doesn't self-actualize, either.

Actually, that's the whole point. Each one of these characters is caught between various psychological forces. For Jack in *Lord of the Flies*, it's power vs. fairness. For Winston Smith, it's self-reliance vs. submission. For Tom Wingfield, it's responsibility vs. freedom.

Each one of them must make a choice that defines their character. Ultimately, each one is offered the road towards self-discovery and ultimately self-actualization.

Each one fails. But now it's the reader's turn. *He can look at this failed journey and take the lessons for himself. He can explore, delve, and learn...oh my!*

Someone once said, "A smart man learns from his own mistakes, but a wise man learns from the mistakes of others." (Maybe that was my dad...or maybe Socrates. I don't know.)

And that's why we read literature.

CHAPTER FOUR

UNCLE FREUD READS SHAKESPEARE...
And Other Stories

Have you ever done something *completely* out of character...something you utterly regretted later--and then wondered *WHAT WAS I THINKING??*

How long has it been since you did something like that? (You might have to look at the clock.)

Sigmund Freud (a name you can't escape in an introductory psych class) has some interesting theories about these "inexplicable" things--theories that can help us dig deeper into the minds of literary characters.

Freud was one controversial dude--and not everybody agrees with some of his disturbing theories. BUT his biggest contribution is his pointing out the power of the *unconscious* forces in the mind.

Shortly before he lived in the early twentieth century, a popular theory called phrenology suggested our personalities were determined by the bumps on our heads.

Crazy, right?

So when Freud came along later and said our behavior is strongly influenced by the parts of our mind that we cannot control, people paid attention. This seemed more logical.

Theory of the Unconscious

What is the unconscious part of the mind? The part beneath the depths. The part that causes us to dream, according to Freud. The part shaped by our early childhood experiences.

It's like the large part of an iceberg that lies below the water. The conscious part of the mind is just the part that sticks out--the part you can see. But that's just a small part.

The unconscious is the larger part of the iceberg below--in the murky depths. Freud said this is hugely influential in our behaviors. Furthermore, he said the mind is made up of three parts: Id, Superego, and Ego.

The *id* is the instinctual part of the mind that operates on the "pleasure principle." It seeks immediate gratification. It

54

wants what it wants, and it wants it now. It's the toddler in our mind, always wanting a cookie. It's spontaneous and fun, but it's also completely selfish, highly sexual, and demanding-- much like your dog when he latches onto your leg in an amorous embrace.

The superego balances this out. It's the Church Lady inside our mind. (If you don't get that reference, watch old episodes of *SNL*.) Highly moral and demanding of perfection, the superego operates on the "morality" principle. It always reminds you to think of the consequences: *Whatever you do, don't eat that cookie!*

It's a big wet blanket. Whenever the id is having a good time, the superego wants it to stop, do its homework, and go to bed. Now!

So who regulates these two diametrically opposing forces, according to Freud? The *ego*. He's the CEO of the mind. He operates on the "reality" principle, listens to the counsel of the id and superego, and then decides who wins.

This fits in well with our opposing forces theory in Chapter One. And to emphasize: Freud believed that our early childhood experiences were HUGELY influential in driving our behaviors.

Much of the id and superego lie within the realm of the unconscious. And they are largely shaped by our early childhood experiences. This is Freud's psychoanalytic view.

BINGO! Now, we can examine the behaviors of our unwitting literary characters through a psychoanalytic lens.

Let's start with Abigail Williams of *The Crucible*. We all know this seventeen year-old girl had an affair with married John Proctor. But why? Was is it his good looks and rugged masculinity? Maybe. But likely there are psychological reasons.

After the Puritan girls are caught dancing in the woods, chaos breaks out. The people suspect witchcraft is afoot. Abigail seizes control of the girls with this threat of violence:

Let either of you breathe a word, or the edge of a word, about the other things, and I will come to you in the black of some terrible night and I will bring a pointy reckoning that will shudder you. And you know I can do it; I saw Indians smash my dear parents' heads on the pillow next to

mine, and I have seen some reddish work done

at night, and I can make you wish you had never

seen the sun go down.

Pretty psychotic, huh? But let's go deeper.

What child would not be traumatized by witnessing the murder of their parents? The result of this tragic event? Abigail is an orphan. She lost her father, and according to Freud, the *relationship between fathers and daughters is critical in their development.*

Shortly after this scene, Abigail is alone with Proctor. Upon seeing him, she exclaims with girlish flirtation, "Gah! I'd almost forgot how strong you are, John Proctor!"

Very revealing! Proctor represents a strong father-like presence in Abigail's life, one that has been missing since her early childhood. Is she aware of this? Maybe. Maybe not. More likely her attraction to the strapping farmer is driven by her Freudian unconscious desires.

We could also bring Maslow into this. Proctor's strength of body and mind feeds Abigail's need for safety and love and belonging. Again, something conspicuously absent since her childhood.

We could say then that Abigail struggles between the opposing psychological forces of **paternal love** and **puritanical propriety**. The sad result is the death of lots of innocent people, including John Proctor.

This reveals yet another psychological dynamic. The struggles within our minds (often on the unconscious level) often manage to take physical form in the result of violence. Pepper Lewis says, "Wars are the reenactments of the battles that rage in the minds of humans."

So what starts as a conflict in the depths of Abigail Williams' mind ultimately manifests in the bodies of innocent people swinging from the gallows.

That's some heavy stuff.

Now, let's visit a more lighthearted character: Huckleberry Finn. What do we know about Huck's early childhood? Very little. But wait! We know that he has an abusive drunk of a father and his mother was M.I.A. during his childhood. We know nothing about her...she is never mentioned in Huck's life.

Precisely! Her absence is a huge void! According to Freud, *the relationship between mothers and sons has a profound effect on the boy's relationship with women later in life.*

Huckleberry is an astute con man. He can lie his socks off to get out of a jam. Nobody can construct a more detailed convincing lie than Huck!

Unless he's lying to one type of person: *a woman.*

He lies badly to Mrs. Loftus, Susan the "harelip," and to Aunt Sally. As a result, they catch him in a web of lies. If it's a man involved (Pap Finn, the King and Duke, Jim, the slave bounty hunters, etc.), Huck lies impressively. But not for a woman. This causes his superego to win the battle against his id.

Coincidence? I think not.

Using Freud's theory of psychoanalysis, we could say the lack of a female presence in his life leads to his anxious feelings around women. With each of the female cases, Huck gets flustered and tongue-tied. Freud believed that sexual conflict drives much of human behavior. This belief has drawn the ire of many of his critics, but it is a cornerstone of Freudian psychoanalysis.

Because Freud's theories were so popular in the early to mid-twentieth century, they often show up in the literature of that period. In Aldous Huxley's *Brave New World*, the id and superego are reversed. In this dystopian world, promiscuity is considered moral behavior. Even children are encouraged to participate in sexual play with each other. Women carry contraceptives with them everywhere they go because they have sex with nearly every man they meet.

If a woman sleeps with only one man for a length of time, she is considered immoral and indecent. Suppression of human desire is considered unhealthy and unnatural. Huxley ingeniously makes us question the nature of morality by spinning Freud's depiction of the id and superego.

The point to remember:

Since most novels and stories deal with morality and social mores on some level, you can use Freud's terms (id, ego, and superego) as tools to explain moral behavior.

The Oedipal Complex & Freudian Symbols

Now it's time to discuss the darker side of Freud's theories: the Oedipal Complex. Freud believed that children are attracted to their opposite sex parent. In other words, a boy feels attraction to his mother and sees his father as competition for her affection. The name is taken from Oedipus Rex, the King of Thebes who married his mother and killed his father.

According to Freud, this psychological dynamic drives a man to seek a woman who reminds him of his mother. And that leads us to everybody's favorite Dane and classic over-thinker: Hamlet.

Freud believed that Hamlet was actually torn between the opposing forces of desire for his mother and societal mores. To illustrate: In Act III Hamlet enters his mother's bedroom with a sword. Filled with rage, he accuses her of grave wrongdoing by marrying her dead husband's brother Claudius.

In Freud's view, Hamlet's speech is actually a disguise for his hidden desire for his mother (in the bedroom, no less). And the sword is a phallic symbol for Hamlet's sexual rage.

Disturbing? You bet it is. But you can find other phallic symbols in literature.

The Glass Menagerie's Laura Wingfield has an obsession with unicorns. She was abandoned by her father and is terrified of men.

Why a unicorn, of all creatures? Why not a horse?

The unicorn has an obvious phallic symbol, which represents the traumatic experience of Laura being abandoned by the most important male in her life. It's no coincidence that Jim (Laura's love interest) breaks the horn off the unicorn and makes it "normal,"--like all the rest of the horses.

Then there's the killing of the pig in *Lord of the Flies*. Jack and his crew attack and kill a mother pig with lustful violence:

Here, struck down by the heat, the sow fell and
the hunters hurled themselves at her. This
dreadful eruption from an unknown world made
her frantic; she squealed and bucked and the air
was full of sweat and noise and blood and terror
[...]. The spear moved forward inch by inch and

the terrified squealing became a high-pitched

scream. Then Jack found the throat and the hot

blood spouted over his hands. The sow collapsed

under them….

This is deeply Freudian behavior. On the surface, it's a quest for food. But on the unconscious level, it mirrors a rape scene of a mother, using a very prominent phallic symbol.

Dark and sinister? Yes.

Does the Oedipal complex show up in most stories? No. But the bottom line is this:

> **Pay attention to anything about your literary character's childhood. You may be able to use it to explain unconscious behavior.**

If called upon to justify your explanation, you can say, "Sigmund Freud says so!" Just be sure to say it while smoking a cigar (Freud was famous for those.)

CHAPTER FIVE

THOSE PESKY ARCHETYPES

Saved By the Bell is one of my all-time favorite TV shows. Generations of teens have connected with its loveable characters: Zack Morris, Kelly Kapowski, AC Slater, Screech, Lisa Turtle, and Jessie Spano.

Why?

Let's face it. Haven't we all gone to school with a prep, a cheerleader, jock, geek, etc? Every high school of America has a cocky Zack Morris with the world as his oyster. We've all met a loveable, awkward Screech who somehow never gets the girl.

These are called ***archetypes***, a psychological term used by the Swiss psychologist Carl Jung. These are basically stock characters who can be found in nearly all of literature.

Archetypes share similar qualities or traits. Jung identified a few specific categories, and other folks have added to the list. Let's look at a few examples, and I'll bet you can think of some of your own.

But first, I should mention why archetypes exist, according to Jung. He developed the theory of the **collective unconscious**, which is the collective mind of humanity. He defined this as the reservoir for human experiences, which are passed along from one generation to the next.

Here's the rationale: you inherit genes for your physical body from your parents, grandparents, and so on...right? Jung theorized that you also inherit psychological baggage from your ancestors. This means that your behavior can be influenced not only by your experiences, but by the experiences from your family tree. (Neuroscience has proven much of this to be true.)

What does this have to do with archetypes? Jung believed that archetypes (or templates for characters in the human story) are passed along from one generation to the next via the collective unconscious.

Archetypes aid in our understanding of our "tension of opposites." Jung said the goal of the collective unconscious is to guide people to growth, or "self-individuation."

Now, we know that growth does not occur without conflict, or tension of opposites. Right?

So there we are. If we can identify archetypes in literature, we can examine *how* they contribute to the psychological conflicts and growth of our characters.

Once you identify the archetypes, use these probing tools for further psychological analysis. I'll call these the **BIG BOX QUESTIONS:**

> 1. *What tension of opposites exist around this archetype?*
>
> 2. *How does this archetype impact the growth of others in the story? ("Others" can include your protagonist, antagonist, secondary characters, or more importantly...the READER.)*

Enough of my chatter. Here are Jung's archetypes:

The Hero

This is your big, strapping character, known for his brawn, who saves the day. He can also be unusually smart, but muscles seem to be a big factor. The archetypal hero is often part-man, part-god who makes some kind of sacrifice for the greater good.

Odysseus is one of the early prototypes. He's the only one strong enough to bend the bow used to launch arrows through the axe handle sockets, but it's really his analytical thinking that gets him out of jams. He employs his creative thinking to outsmart the cyclops, for example.

Odysseus is constantly assailed with the opposing forces of cerebral thought vs. reflexive action (or action vs. reaction). And it's his use of his prefrontal cortex that wins the day.

Not only does he grow from his conflicts, but hopefully the reader does, as well.

Achilles from *The Iliad* is another archetypal hero. Definitely more on the brawn side. When Hector kills his best friend Patroclus, Achilles sees red. Mortal combat must ensue. (Not the video game...the real kind--although a virtual battle might have been better.)

Achilles finds himself smack dab in the middle of the conflict rage vs. justice. Brawn vs. brain.

Of course, rage wins. An eye for an eye is not enough for Achilles. After killing Hector, he drags the body with horses in full view of Hector's father and fellow Trojans.

68

Does the punishment fit the crime? You decide. But the discussion of this universal conflict should lead to growth of some sort.

If you're a fan of superheroes, virtually all of them are variants of the archetypal hero. We don't have time to discuss all of them, but the biggies, like Superman, Spiderman, Batman, Wonder Woman, and Black Panther often find themselves in psychological conflicts.

The next time you pick up a comic book, look for those opposing forces and ask those big-box questions.

The Child

Often in literature, you find a kid who doesn't act like a kid. In fact, he or she is usually more adult-like in behavior. Often difficult to control and your basic nightmare for the parents, this is the archetypal child.

Pearl in *The Scarlet Letter* is a classic example. She is the result of her mother's adulterous affair with Arthur Dimmesdale. The product of sin. And she enjoys reminding her mother of this fact.

When Pearl asks her mother where she came from, Hester replies, "Thy heavenly father sent thee."

Not buying it, Pearl retorts, "I have no heavenly father!"

Ouch. What a little wild child!

Pearl seems to know things that a normal child would not. She struggles with opposing forces of abandonment vs. love. On one side is her father who refuses (for most of the novel) to acknowledge his daughter. On the other side is a little girl who just wants to be held by her daddy.

Also, Pearl certainly presents opposing forces for her parents. But hey, what kid doesn't do that? Someone famous once said, "Out of the mouth of babes" the truth emerges.

The child archetype is often cartoonish in nature. Maybe that's why it shows up in cartoons like Calvin in *Calvin & Hobbes*, Bart Simpson, or Stewie Griffin in *The Family Guy*. Be on the lookout for this stock character. Again, they offer psychological depth if you ask the Big Box questions.

The Wise Old Man

Ever notice how many Gandalfs are out there? You know the type: an old, wizened man, usually with long, flowy whiskers, who dispenses wisdom to the protagonist or other

70

characters. He might come in different flavors and colors, but at heart he's the archetypal wise old man.

Since most people know the obvious ones--like Gandalf, Obi wan Kenobi, and Dumbledore--let's look at a lesser known one: Professor Pangloss from *Candide*.

Pangloss (whose name means "all talk") believes that everything happens for a reason. He's an eternal optimist whose views run contrary to most of Candide's tragic experiences. You see the opposing forces here, right? Optimism vs. cynicism. Idealism vs. realism.

And that's the whole point. Voltaire uses the archetypal wise old man to parody the philosophy of optimism. Jung believed this archetype exists in the collective unconscious because each person has access to it. We all just need to tap into our resident wise old man to find solutions to our problems.

Just as Odysseus goes to blind old Tiresias for guidance, all of us--including our literary friends--can connect with this powerful force.

Remember bumper cars at the theme park? You and your friends got into different cars and drove around, ramming each other at every chance. And you never knew which direction you would bounce into.

Apply this principle to your wise old man. Be on the lookout for any wise character (male or female) and watch how he rams your protagonist and sends him flying into a new direction. In other words: identify the psychological impact.

The Trickster

According to Jung, the trickster can be a man or god who disobeys the normal rules for behavior. Often mischievous, he enjoys creating havoc for others. Puck, from *A Mid-Summer Night's Dream* comes to mind. This "shrewd and knavish sprite" creates delightful chaos by pouring his magic love potion on his sleeping victims, causing them to fall in love with the first one they see upon awakening. Puck's biggest laugh comes when Tatiana, the fairy queen, wakes up and falls in love with a donkey.

Tricksters show up often in folklore, mythology, cartoons, comic books, etc.--probably due to their supernatural tendencies. A few other examples are Rumplestiltskin, Loki, Bugs Bunny, the Joker (I'll bet you can keep the list going).

Although some tricksters may have their own tension of opposites, sometimes they are flat characters (i.e., uni-dimensional). In that case, they often serve as a catalyst to your protagonist's quest. They may ram into him, sending him flying into all directions.

If this happens, direct your psychological analysis to your protagonist. The trickster is applying the heat, so the protagonist is the one who must deal with opposing forces and grow.

For example, Hermes (the messenger of the gods in *The Odyssey*) warns Odysseus that Circe has changed his men into animals. Hermes then offers Odysseus a magic herb that will protect him from her powers. Here, the opposing forces act upon Odysseus, with the trickster acting as a catalyst for his growth.

Now, we don't see magic herbs and fairies in real life, so what's the point of the trickster? Why is it so common in literature?

A fair question.

Since the characters and conflicts in literature are essentially projections of our own psychological struggles, the trickster represents the unpredictability and silliness that can fall out of the sky and just land in our lap. We don't seem to have control over it...it all just seems crazy and haphazard. Fun, frivolity, and mishaps can be great ways to learn and connect with our own humanity, too

And after laughing at the insanity of it all, we can say, "Hey, I actually grew from this experience!"

Just ask Odysseus.

CHAPTER SIX

MENTAL DISORDERS

Who's your favorite villain?

Lex Luther? Professor Snape? Anakin Skywalker? Plankton?

Ever wonder WHY he's your personal fave? For some folks, the more outlandish, the more psychotic, the more unexplainable the behavior...the better. Yes, we have a fascination with characters who do horrible things we would never *dream* of doing! And if we tried to imitate their behavior, I'm pretty sure we'd get locked up in a jail cell or a psychiatric ward.

And that leads to our main question: Are these characters mentally ill?

And how else can an understanding of mental disorders help us in analyzing literature?

Glad you asked. First, let's take a look at how mental disorders are defined. There's a book called *The Diagnostic and Statistical Manual of Mental Disorders* (known as the *DSM*), which is the authoritative guide--some call it the bible--for mental illnesses. At the time of this writing, it's in the fifth edition.

Any time a psychiatrist, psychologist, or therapist diagnoses a person with a mental illness, that person must meet the checklist of traits listed in the *DSM*. For example, if a person is diagnosed with clinical depression (one of the most common mental disorders), he/she must have had the condition for at least two weeks, according to the *DSM-V*.

There are so many moments in literature when a character seems depressed--in the clinical sense. The more we know about depression, the more we can analyze and understand the behavior of our unfortunate character.

And since depression is so common in our culture, let's start with this mental disorder and see how it manifests in literature. Then we'll extend our exploration to other literary mental disorders.

Ready to explore the darkness? Got your flashlight? Here we go...

DEPRESSION

In *Man's Search for Meaning*, Viktor Frankl describes his experiences as a Holocaust survivor. As a psychiatrist and a prisoner in the death camps, he was able to use his skills to help his fellow Jews. The Nazis used "selection," in which they decided who would be used for labor and who would be sent to their deaths.

Hope was critical for these prisoners. If they allowed themselves to slip into depression, their physical health would decline--practically a guarantee they would be selected for the gas chamber. As a psychiatrist, Frankl knew this and worked hard to encourage others.

Although nonfiction, this book reveals an important dynamic in the literary world of fictional characters. **Depression can be life or death for characters.** If not physical death, then an emotional or metaphorical death.

But the effects of depression may not stop there. Oftentimes, depressed characters will act out in very negative ways, lashing out at others through their psychological pain. As Carl Jung said, "It is not the healthy man who tortures others--generally it is the tortured who turn into torturers."

This is especially helpful in analyzing the characterization of villains.

So what are the traits to look for? Using the DSM-V as our guide, clinical depression has the following traits:

- Depressed mood most of the day
- Loss of interest in activities that normally bring about pleasure
- Loss of appetite or significant weight loss
- Insomnia or hypersomnia (sleeping too much)
- Psychomotor agitation (restlessness, pacing, slowed speech, quiet talking)
- Fatigue nearly every day
- Feelings of worthlessness or guilt
- Inability to concentrate or make decisions
- Recurrent thoughts of death

If you come across a character with several of these traits, depression could be an underlying force acting upon him. Of course, we know that *one force always has its opposite force*, and we could use Maslow's theory of human needs to identify that opposite force.

Let's start with Miss Havisham of *Great Expectations*. This poor wretch was deserted at the altar and spends the rest of her days holed up in a dark room with windows drawn, clothed in her wedding dress, while her old wedding cake rots on the table. All the clocks in her house are stopped at the moment she was jilted at the altar.

The joy of life now completely sucked out of her, Miss Havisham is one sad, pitiful sack. (You can quote me on that.) She clearly displays signs of clinical depression, so let's analyze the conflict that produced the depression and its effect.

The psychological conflict of Miss Havisham is a combination of two opposing forces. Being jilted at the altar is one force--and clearly a negative one at that. What's the opposing force? (Think Maslow.) Her need for love and belonging from her would-be husband.

This conflict is what leads to her clinical depression-- which, in turn, creates her dysfunctional behavior. In addition to living as a bitter hermit, she vows revenge against the male gender. For this purpose, she adopts Estella and grooms her into a haughty, beautiful femme fatale, capable of wreaking

havoc on the hearts of men--most notably Pip's. Poor kid--
he just wants to be loved like everybody else.

Let's apply a simple three-part procedure to explore the
dynamics around the depression and how it impacts the
character's life. (You can use this method to explore any
conflict, mind you.)

BIG BOX QUESTIONS

Q #1	What *negative experience* does the character have?
Q #2	What *human need* does the character have?
Q#3	How does the character respond to this struggle?

Just remember that Force #1 tends to be the unpleasant
force, whereas Force #2 tends to be the basic human need
that counters it. The effect can be psychological, physical, or
both.

Now, let's try this on Herman Melville's "Bartleby the
Scrivener." Just a heads-up: this is one creepy dude...

Bartleby works in a corporate office when seemingly out
of the blue, he refuses anything and everything. Whenever
his boss asks him to do something, his response is "I'd prefer

80

not to." Amazingly, his boss doesn't fire him because he pities the poor, pale, emaciated Bartleby. (You see what I did with the alliteration?)

When everyone leaves the office at the end of the day, Bartleby refuses to go. "I'd prefer not to" becomes his refrain for *everything*: he refuses to go home, he refuses to take care of himself...he even refuses to eat! In this regard, he refuses to live and will surely die.

Bartleby fits the pattern for clinical depression. Suicide by non-action.

Using the Big Box questions, what do we find?

Q #1: *What negative experience led to Bartleby's state?* We discover that Bartleby used to work for the "Dead Letters Office." This was a department of mail delivery that dealt with returned letters from dead recipients. The narrator of the story wonders how many times Bartleby had to be reminded of death on a daily basis. Evidently, this had a profound effect on him, reminding him of the brevity and futility of life (at least in Melville's perspective...he was a pretty dark thinker).

Q #2: *What human need is beneath Bartleby's depression?* Human connection and a sense of safety. Bartleby seems very much alone. If he had a network of emotional support, he'd be less likely to give up. He needs the love of family and friends to feel safe in a difficult and unpredictable world. He also needs to feel that life has meaning, and that is very difficult when a person feels detached and alone.

Q#3: *How does Bartleby respond?* By giving up on life. He basically says, "I quit doing anything!" The story ends with the narrator visiting Bartleby in an asylum, where he finds him curled up on the floor, emaciated and withering away in his refusal to eat. Death is imminent, leading to Melville's pessimistic pronouncement: "Ah, Bartleby! Ah, humanity!" Bartleby's depression ultimately kills him. He doesn't rise above it, and an astute reader will see this as a warning for us all: *depression can kill*.

Bartleby is a good example, but my Saddest Sack Award goes to Victor Frankenstein of his eponymous novel (go look up that word). Let's use our Big Box questions on our brilliant, yet emotionally depleted scientist...

Q#1: *What is Victor's negative experience?* After Victor abandons the monster at "birth," his creation goes on a killing spree, targeting Victor's family and friends: William, Justine, Henry, Elizabeth, etc. The acting forces here are violence, mayhem, and murder.

Q#2: *What opposing need does Victor have?* Clearly, Victor's need for love of family and friends and his genuine concern for humanity (i,e., needs for love/belonging) drive his quest for justice.

Q#3: *How does Victor respond to this clash of forces?* Psychologically, the conflict throws Victor into deep depression: he is "tempted to plunge into the silent lake, that the waters might close over me and my calamities forever." He even begs nature, "Oh! Stars, and clouds, and winds...if ye really pity me, crush sensation and memory; let me become as nought, but if not, depart, depart, and leave me in darkness."

Physically, this conflict drives Victor to chase the monster down in an effort to kill him. Alas, Victor's quest remains unfulfilled, as he dies of cold and exhaustion in the far North. No doubt, his depression was a contributor to his death. So let that be a lesson to the kids out there. If not, just remember: *be nice to monsters, especially if they're eight-feet tall.*

ANXIETY DISORDERS

We're an anxious society, wouldn't you say? Maybe that's why anxiety disorders are the most common mental illnesses in our culture. And likewise in literature, you could probably find lots of stressed out characters.

Actually, anxiety disorders come in different types: *Panic Disorder*, *Social Anxiety Disorder*, and *General Anxiety Disorder*. Let's take each one and find a literary example.

People with **Panic Disorder** have feelings of terror that strike suddenly and repeatedly with no warning. Other symptoms of a panic attack include sweating, chest pain, palpitations (unusually strong or irregular heartbeats), and a feeling of choking. It can feel like you're having a heart attack or "going crazy."

This sounds like nearly every narrator in an Edgar Allan Poe story! But for our purposes, let's discuss one of his most famous and beloved stories: "The Tell-Tale Heart."

The narrator shows his anxiety in the opening lines:

"True! --nervous --very, very dreadfully nervous I had been and am; but why will you say that I am mad?"

But it gets worse.

After murdering his landlord and hiding the body parts beneath the floorboards, the narrator becomes increasingly agitated:

The officers were satisfied. My manner had convinced them. I was singularly at ease. They sat, and while I answered cheerily, they chatted of familiar things. But, ere long, I felt myself getting pale and wished them gone. My head ached, and I fancied a ringing in my ears: but still they sat and still chatted. The ringing became more distinct: --It continued and became more distinct: I talked more freely to get rid of the feeling: but it continued and gained definiteness --until, at length, I found that the noise was not within my ears. No doubt I now grew very pale; --but I talked more fluently, and with a heightened voice. Yet the sound increased--and what could I do? It was a low, dull, quicksound--much such a sound as a watch makes when enveloped in cotton. I gasped for breath --and yet the officers heard it not.

Finally, the narrator's panic attack completely engulfs him...

I felt I must scream or die! And now--again!-hark! louder! louder! louder! louder! 'Villains!' I shrieked, dissemble no more! I admit the deed! --tear up the planks! here, here! --It is the beating of his hideous heart!

So what do we have here? A panic disorder for starters.
There may be other mental illnesses as well. (That's called
comorbidity). But we can start with his anxiety. If we knew
more about the character, we could address the Big Box
questions, but we know virtually nothing about the narrator
before or after this incident. However, his symptoms clearly
point to a panic disorder. So when he says early on, "You
fancy me mad. Mad men know nothing," he is clearly
unaware or in denial of his mental illness.

Social Anxiety Disorder, or "social phobia," causes a
person to feel overwhelmingly self-conscious in ordinary
social situations. This person is terrified to go out in the world
for fear of being judged or ridiculed by others.

No, this is not your typical middle school experience. We
were all self-conscious back then. But the person with social
anxiety disorder has the fear to such a degree that he cannot
function in the world. A trip to the grocery store or movies
would paralyze him.

This sounds a lot like Boo Radley of *To Kill a
Mockingbird*. Boo rarely sets foot outside of his house and is
seen as some kind of aberration by the folks of Maycomb

County. Jem and Scout think he's a horrifying monster, but the truth is that Boo is simply misunderstood.

The underlying force behind Boo's reclusion lies in his past. As a youth, he got himself into legal trouble and was sentenced to either jail or house arrest. His family chose the latter, but he seems to be emotionally neglected by his family.

The obvious force leading to his dysfunction is his family's neglect. People with social anxiety disorder do not feel emotionally safe, loved, or valued. There's no evidence that Boo was truly cared for by his father or the rest of his family. His human need for love and belonging is what pulls on this neglect in his psychological tug of war.

How does Boo respond to this conflict? For most of his life, it is social withdrawal. But at the end of the novel, he makes the conscious choice to rise above the anxiety, rush out of his house, and save Jem and Scout from the violent hands of Mr. Ewell.

Boo is a hero. Not only for saving the children, but by saying "Enough!" to his social anxiety for the sake of others. He challenges his fearful view of the world, rolls the dice, and wins. In short, his love conquers his fear.

General Anxiety Disorder

Some characters seem to be constantly on edge, even seemingly for no reason. If they suffer with *General Anxiety Disorder*, they have excessive, unrealistic worry--even when there's little or nothing to provoke the anxiety. These folks seem to be in constant "fight, flight, or freeze mode" unnecessarily.

You may be thinking of someone you know right now, but for an illustration let's visit the world of *The Glass Menagerie*. Laura Wingfield is a young lady who apparently suffers with GAD. (Egads!) She lives in a poor apartment with her fussy mother Amanda and her brother Tom, the sole supporter of his family.

Crippled with low self-esteem and constant anxiety, Laura has no means to support herself. Her mother tried enrolling her in a business class to learn a trade, but poor Laura vomited on the day of a test and quit school. She can't function out in the world and prefers staying home to play with her glass animal collection while playing old records given to her by her father.

88

When Amanda forces Tom to invite some poor schmuck to dinner to meet Laura in hopes of landing her a husband, Laura is so terrified, she can't sit at the dinner table to eat.

Whew! Laura is overcome with anxiety and cannot function. But why? What's going on with her psychologically?

Using our Big Box questions, let's look at some of her opposing forces. What event could have contributed to her general anxiety disorder? Aside from her henpecking mother, Laura's father deserted the family when she was very young. All he left her was the old records she now plays when she gets stressed out.

The relationship between a father and daughter is critical to her emotional development, so Laura was abandoned (cast away, if you will) by the most important man in her life. No wonder she feels worthless! It doesn't help that she has an old-school mother who constantly talks about how she needs a big, strong man to take care of her!

What psychological force opposes her father's desertion? Her need for safety, love, and affirmation. And how does she respond to this emotional conflict? Whenever she feels overwhelmed (which is often!), she plays those old records that her father left her. In other words, she enters a world that reminds her of her missing father.

Also, she plays with her glass animals--most notably the unicorn, her favorite. Freud would probably have a field day interpreting that predilection, but you decide for yourself.

PERSONALITY DISORDERS

Sometimes you encounter a character whose personality "just ain't right." In other words, these folks could use a big attitude adjustment. Well, hold your horses because psychology has names for these personality peccadilloes.

A *personality disorder* occurs when a person has deeply embedded habits and patterns of behavior that keeps him from functioning in society. The DSM-V lists 10 different ones, but for our purposes, we're going to discuss the most prevalent. First up is…

Paranoid Personality Disorder

This person is constantly suspicious of other people and suspects they have sinister motives. He often searches for hidden meanings in everyday occurrences and is often cold and distant. He always places blame on someone else and carries longstanding grudges. For this reason, he just can't seem to have authentic intimate relationships.

We already mentioned the narrator of "The Tale-Tell Heart" as a candidate for panic disorder. He also demonstrates the traits above. His poor landlord did nothing to deserve his suspicions, hostility, and violence, right? Since the narrator probably has more than one mental illness, we say that his paranoid personality disorder is *comorbid* with his panic disorder--remember that term?

Honestly, lots of Poe's characters seem to suffer from comorbid mental conditions. Take Roderick from "The Fall of the House of Usher," for example. This poor guy is hit from all directions. Aside from being deeply anxious and depressed, he thinks his house may be a living, breathing entity, and feels the need to murder his poor innocent sister, Madeline.

Roderick is deeply paranoid of everything around him and may very well suffer from paranoid personality disorder. Unfortunately, he perishes beneath the rubble of his house before anyone can get him psychiatric care.

What is a possible source of his paranoia and other conditions? The narrator tells us this chilling fact: "I had learned, too, the very remarkable fact, that the stem of the Usher race, all time-honoured as it was, had put forth, at no period, any enduring branch; in other words, that the entire family lay in the direct line of descent."

Did you get that? Roderick and his twin sister are the products of generations of inbreeding.

Okay. 'Nuff said.

And to follow the cause and effect of the mental illness(es), we can say the ultimate result is two dead twins and a big heaping pile of house rubble.

Onward and upward, I always say.

Antisocial Personality Disorder

Now for the biggie. We've all encountered a villain who just seems like pure evil (no, I'm not talking about your little brother). And we wonder how in the world someone can be that mean. In the past, we often called a person like this a psychopath, and yes, *psychopathy* used to be an accepted term for this condition.

92

But later the term evolved into *sociopathy*, so it became acceptable to refer to this character as a sociopath. But somehow, that term became unpalatable, which leads us to the current term for a person with no conscience: *Antisocial Personality Disorder* (APD).

People with this condition do not feel guilt or remorse. Such emotions are alien to them. As a result, they tend to be psychological predators, believing that others are weak and deserve to be taken advantage of. In fact, they often derive pleasure in causing others pain. Nice, huh?

Oh, yes...they also tend to lie. A lot! It comes easy for them because they feel no guilt and have no empathy for others. Their penchant for lying also enables them to go undetected by others. In fact, they can appear very charming and nice...but look out! They're doing it to manipulate for their own diabolical purposes.

Let's start with Roger Chillingworth of *The Scarlet Letter*. His trophy wife Hester was taken sexually by another man, one Arthur Dimmesdale. Big mistake for him! Dimmesdale is not the most observant guy in the world, so he doesn't notice

Chillingworth's subterfuge, and even becomes besties with the guy, inviting him to live under the same roof.

Chillingworth thoroughly enjoys making Reverend Dimmesdale squirm by asking all kinds of theological questions about guilt and secret sin. He knows that Dimmesdale committed adultery. He knows that he is tormented by guilt. And Chillingworth LOVES IT! Yes, he delights in seeing a tormented soul!

While Dimmesdale is napping, Chillingworth opens his shirt and sees a big "A" carved on his chest. And what does he do? Dances a jig for joy!

Nice guy.

He could have just done the normal thing and punched Dimmesdale in the chops and called it a day. But no, he never wants the punishment to end, and even begs Dimmesdale not to confess on the scaffold at the end of the novel.

Psychopath? Sociopath? Antisocial Personality Disorder? You betcha.

But wait, we're not done with Chillingworth. We need to ask some Big Box questions to see how his tension of opposites interplays with his mental illness.

First, what is the cause of his antisocial personality disorder? What clash of forces may have spawned it? Psychologists don't know the exact causes of this disorder, but suspect that genetics and environment are culprits. APD folks often lacked nurturing parental connections in their early childhood. In other words, they were psychologically isolated.

Now, we know nothing of Chillingworth's childhood, but his isolated environment seems to be fertile soil for his disease. One driving force in his life is his intrinsic desire for knowledge. This leads him to spend years in the wilderness learning medical secrets from Native Americans. My hunch is that he did not form lasting relationships there.

The other force clashing with his intellectual drive is his natural human need for love and belonging. Yes, he had a wife, but didn't live with her. He never gave or drew warmth from that relationship. The bottom line is he chose the path of the intellect while abandoning his emotional needs, and his antisocial personality disorder likely grew from this.

Second, what is the ultimate effect of Chillingworth's APD? Aside from tormenting poor Dimmesdale, Roger dies shortly after Dimmesdale's death, so we can safely assume he never self-actualized. In other words, he never reached his full potential for growth as a human being. His APD leads to an early, lonely and miserable death.

But hey...that's Hawthorne!

I'd like to nominate some other characters for the APD Award, but leave you to ponder the analysis of each. Here are a few other friendly, neighborhood sociopaths:

Abigail Williams--*The Crucible*

Jack--*Lord of the Flies*

O'Brien--*1984*

Claggart--*Billy Budd*

I'm sure you could add to this list. Whomever you choose, extend your analysis with these three easy baking tips...

> 1. Explore how the environment might lead to the disorder.
>
> 1. Identify the clash of forces extending from their human needs.
>
> 2. Pinpoint the outcome.

Borderline Personality Disorder

Now for your drama queens. Some characters always seem to generate drama and controversy. Their default attitude towards all problems is "I'm the victim! You're to blame!"--even though they are usually the culprit. They never take ownership of their own psychological problems, growth, or emotional well being. That's someone else's job.

Such characters may have *Borderline Personality Disorder* (BPD). First, let's clarify the name. "Borderline" doesn't mean they are on the border of having the disorder; it means they border on full-blown psychological breakdown.

BPD folks have extremely fast mood changes. They can go from zero to sixty in a heartbeat. One second, they seem perfectly normal. The next, they're screaming bloody murder.

Aside from the explosive anger, they also have unstable relationships, feelings of emptiness, and poor self-esteem. Sometimes, they even engage in self-harm.

They always seem to be at the center of a conflict. No one in their circle of friends or family are safe from their blame game. And most frustrating is their inability to see their role or responsibility in these conflicts. It's always the other person's fault.

Whew! No wonder BPD characters are drama queens! Now, let's explore some examples...

Pride and Prejudice ranks right up there with *Mean Girls* and *The Notebook* as a right of passage for female adolescence. And if you're male, fear not! It's hidden subtitle is "Everything You Wanted to Know About Women, But Were Afraid to Ask."

Just kidding.

But not really.

Our heroine Elizabeth Bennet is one of five daughters in the Bennet family. More than *anything else* in this whole wide world, her mother wants each daughter married to a big, strong rich white guy. (This is early 1800's England, mind you.)

Let's zero in on Lizzie's mother. Mrs. Bennet is a constant worrier. Her incessant agitation stresses out everyone else in the household. This includes Mr. Bennet, Jane, Elizabeth, Mary, Catherine, and Lydia.

And here's why: all five of her daughters MUST be married! ASAP! No time for delay! The sky is falling, and the only solution is five weddings with all her daughters exchanging nuptials. That's how she thinks, anyway. Here are some examples...

First, she wants Jane to marry the wealthy socialite Mr. Bingley. So much that she's willing to send Jane over to his house sick so she can trap him into feeling sorry for her, taking care of her, falling in love with her--and then marry her. Simple plan of execution, right?

Next, she wants Elizabeth to marry her cousin Collins. Yes, I know: *Ick!* But that's how it went down in England during the nineteenth century. It was actually very common for cousins to marry. When Elizabeth turns down his marriage proposal, Mrs. Bennet goes postal.

She also wants marriage for the other daughters, when they're old enough. And Mrs. Bennet is leaving nothing to chance! Her life mission is to ensure across-the-board marriages!

She constantly bickers her hen-pecked husband and daughters to death. Poor Mr. Bennet often hides in his man-cave (i.e, his study) to get away from her. Her daughters are constantly at odds with her. But here's how Mrs. Bennet sees it all:

Two inferences, however, were plainly deduced from the whole: one, that Elizabeth was the real cause of all the mischief; and the other, that she herself had been barbarously used by them all; and on these two points she principally dwelt during the rest of the day. Nothing could console and nothing would appease her. Nor did that day wear out her resentment. A week elapsed before she could see Elizabeth without scolding her....

The sad truth is that Mrs. Bennet is the center, focal point of all the drama in the family. She puts way too much pressure on everyone to fulfill her demands, and when they do not succeed, she excoriates them. Moreover, she is completely unwilling or unable to see her role in the conflicts-- a hallmark of Borderline Personality Disorder.

Frustrating as she is, Mrs. Bennet can actually draw our sympathy and understanding if we look at the opposing forces surrounding her. During her time period, women were not allowed to inherit property by law. That means when Mr. Bennet dies, his entire estate would go to the nearest male relative, and Mrs. Bennet and her daughters would be poor and penniless, unless each daughter can land a big, wealthy husband.

Opposing this force is the basic needs of her daughters for economic safety and resources. And how does she respond? By pushing her daughters. It may be to the point of extreme, but at least we can understand what is swirling in her mind.

As a possible candidate for BPD, Mrs. Bennet does not grow. She never sees her role in the family dysfunction: she never takes ownership of her actions. Thus, she is a flat, static character whose main contribution is the growth of

Elizabeth, who looks at her mother with disgust and chooses to be the complete opposite.

Histrionic Personality Disorder

Ever meet a character who always must be the center of attention? If he has *histrionic personality disorder*, he's a constant attention seeker. He may be theatrical, egocentric, self-indulgent, and extremely inconsiderate towards the needs of others.

The famous Tom Sawyer has most, if not all, these traits. In *The Adventures of Huckleberry Finn*, Tom forms a gang with the neighborhood kids and then disappears until the end of the novel. And that's where we're treated to his histrionic stunts.

Huck stumbles into the Phelps plantation in search of Jim, his best friend and a runaway slave. Big surprise for Huck: the Phelps are actually Tom's relatives, expecting Tom to show up for a visit. When Tom arrives, we are treated to a fireworks display of his histrionic personality.

Huck simply wants to free Jim, who is imprisoned in a shed in the back of the Phelps' place. But nooo...Tom won't have it! He quickly commandeers the situation and makes it all about him. He forces Huck to pretend that they are pirates trying to free a royal prisoner, and then makes poor Jim suffer needlessly by filling his cell with rats and snakes and making him sleep on a rock floor.

Then Tom chains Jim to the bed, and then nearly gets poor Jim shot when Tom leaves a warning note to the Phelps that Pirates are coming to break Jim out.

Why does Tom do all this? It seems completely superfluous, unnecessary, and basically idiotic. Yes, Tom is an idiot. There's no doubt about that. But his idiocy may result from his incessant need to be the center of attention at all times. He can never let a situation be about anyone else. He *must* have the spotlight.

When the no-nonsense Huckleberry asks Tom why on earth he did all this, Tom says,
"If we got Jim out all safe…[we'd] take him home on a steamboat...and have them waltz him into town with a torchlight procession and a brass-band, and then he would be a hero, and so would we."

Tom is a pretty vacuous character. Not a lot of depth in that pool. He's entertaining, fun, but never really grows. And sadly, that's a result of his histrionic tendencies. He sacrifices growth for fun.

Narcissistic Personality Disorder

Some personality disorders seem awfully similar to others. *Narcissistic personality disorder* is eerily similar to its histrionic brethren. This character is a self-centered bloke who often exaggerates his achievements, thinking they are superior to everyone else's.

Because Mr. Narcissus thinks so highly of himself, he's very choosy about his friends. Only the best of the best are entitled to his company. Everything is about him, and he cares little for the feelings of others.

In Oscar Wilde's *The Picture of Dorian Gray*, our title character is our leading candidate. Dorian Gray is a handsome young man obsessed with his own beauty. A local artist named Basil paints his portrait while Dorian wishes that the painting would age instead of his own dazzling, chiseled face.

Sure enough, Dorian gets his wish. The years pass, but his face remains the same. This leads Dorian to sink into a path of moral hedonism and debauchery at the gross expense of others. He courts Sibyl Vance, a young actress, then promptly dumps her because he says her acting was the only thing beautiful about her.

When the distraught Sibyl commits suicide, Dorian's only reaction is a shrug of the shoulders. He then goes on to live a sexually indulgent life in opium dens, murders Basil, and leaves a trail of broken hearts.

Undoubtedly, Dorian is king of the narcissists. But what are his psychological battles? In all probability, his narcissistic personality disorder is the result of his need for love and admiration making a head-on collision with his need for growth.

He sacrifices the latter for the former.

And rather than fulfill his need for love with nurturing, healthy relationships, he overcompensates for his emotional hunger by bingeing on carnal desire.

The mental disorders discussed in this chapter are only a few. There are lots, lots more! But they all point to one common principle: *violent behavior nearly always stems from pain.* This concept applies to those characters with mental disorders and those without them. It even applies to us--the readers.

And on that note, violent behavior will leap off the page while you're reading. It's hard to miss. Just remember the violence can be *physical* or *verbal*. You can describe it as violent, dysfunctional, cruel, or whatever you want...but at the end of the day, it's negative behavior.

Once you identify it, start asking those Big Box questions, and you'll find lots of ideas to throw around in class discussions, essays, or just the big area in your head.

Actually, that's our next topic of discussion...

CHAPTER SEVEN

BRAIN STRUCTURES

Back in the early 1990's, a rap group called Cypress Hill hit the charts with their insanely inane song, "Insane in the Brain." Before the song began, a voice gave this warning:

Who you tryin' to get crazy with, ese?
Don't you know I'm loco?

Then later in the chorus, they hit us with this poetic gem:

Insane in the membrane...
Insane in the brain!!
Insane in the membrane...
Crazy insane, got no brain!!

(Sorry if that got stuck in your head. Happens to me every time.)

Now think of our literary friends. Does this mean their dysfunctional human behavior stems from a lack of brains? Of course not. In fact, they have as much brains as you or I (which may not be saying a lot). But it's the *dynamics* of their brains that are the main point. Let's look at some basic structures of the brain and see if we can use them to explain human behavior.

(Plot spoiler: We can.)

We are going to look at the most important basic parts of the brain that could aid in our discussion of literature. In other words, the parts that can be most helpful to understand the actions of our literary characters. Let's begin with the oldest and most basic parts of the brain.

Our brain is the result of thousands of years of evolution. Modern humans have a larger brain than our early ancestors because it grew larger over time with added layers. In fact, a brain looks "wrinkled" because there are so many layers, it must wrinkle up to fit inside the skull. If you stretched it all out, it would be about the size of four sheets of notebook paper!

Think of your brain as a building. You have your foundation, your ascending stories, and your penthouse apartment on top. The entire building rests upon the foundation. If it stands strong, the upper stories are fine. But if the foundation crumbles, look out!

That foundation of our brain is the part in charge of our survival. It has several players. Let's look at a few basic ones:

OLDER STRUCTURE

BRAIN STRUCTURE	FUNCTION
Brainstem	Responsible for automatic survival functions. Oldest part of the brain.
Medulla	Regulates heartbeat and breathing.
Reticular Formation	Controls arousal.
Cerebellum	Coordinates movement and balance. Looks like a "little brain."

Between the oldest and newest part of the brain is the limbic system. (*Limbus* means "border.")

Think of this as the lowest stories of the building. The limbic system has these three structures:

LIMBIC SYSTEM

BRAIN STRUCTURE	FUNCTION
Amygdala	Controls fight-or-flight response. Linked to aggression and fear.
Nucleus Accumbens	Linked to emotion and reward.
Hippocampus	Processes conscious memories.

Some folks call this lower area of our brain the "caveman brain" or "reptile brain." It knows only the language of instinct and survival. Its job is simple: keep us alive. If you want to have a civilized, intelligent discussion, you must get in the elevator and travel several flights to the upper parts of the building (i.e, the top part of the brain).

CEREBRAL CORTEX

The cerebral cortex evolved much later in human history. At the top floor of the brain is the information-processing center. Although it has various parts, the most helpful one for our literary discussions would be the **frontal lobe.** Located at the top (just like the penthouse apartment), just behind your forehead, the frontal lobe is the center of our planning, judgment, and executive functioning.

In our building analogy, if you want to talk with the guy who calls the shots, you take the elevator to the top floor and ask for the CEO. The **prefrontal cortex (PFC)** is the CEO who lives in the frontal lobe. He is in charge of complex cognitive behavior, personality expression, decision-making, and regulating social behavior.

Damage to the frontal lobe (and especially the prefrontal cortex) can radically alter someone's personality. Back in 1848, Phineas Gage was a railroad worker who survived an explosion that drove a metal rod through his skull, causing severe damage to his frontal lobe. His behavior changed significantly. Whereas he had been reserved and mild-mannered before the accident, he afterwards became dishonest, irascible, and profane. In other words, structures of the brain can be used to explain dysfunctional behavior.

See where this is going...?

> **We all know that literary criticism is inherently subjective. At the end of the day, we are left with our arguments and subjective interpretations. However, one principle is empirical and unalterable:**
>
> *Literary characters--no matter their time, place, or culture--experience their conflicts with the same brain structures common to all humanity.*

HOW TO APPLY THIS TO LITERATURE

Let's say you're writing an essay, and you need just a little more sauce. Making a cross-curricular connection between literature and neuroscience could be just what the doctor ordered. For this end, we're going to cite examples of literary characters smack dab in the middle of a conflict (i.e., caught in opposing forces), and then we'll identify what might be going on with their brain activity.

There are lots of other brain structures you could connect to human behavior, but these are the most helpful to connect to literary conflicts. Most of the examples are from commonly read novels in high school English classes, but if you don't find the one you're looking for, fear not.

Simply find a conflict in any major work that depicts the opposing forces of <u>emotion</u> vs. <u>reason</u>. Then use the brain structures listed here that would be connected to both forces. Most often, the conflict of emotion vs. reason is connected to the <u>limbic system</u> vs. the <u>frontal lobe</u>.

The following chart identifies famous moments in literature

when specific brain structures are activated during conflicts.

1984
Amygdala Nucleus Accumbens Hippocampus Frontal Lobe / Prefrontal Cortex
When Winston is haunted by a dream of his childhood in which his mother gives chocolate to him and his brother, Winston's hippocampus cannot let him forget. The chocolate itself appeals to his nucleus accumbens, yet when he steals his brother's portion, his amygdala causes him to flee in terror. --- His frontal lobe is clearly highlighted in his epiphany: *"It was not by making yourself heard but by staying sane that you carried on the human heritage."* This reflective knowledge propels him forward to challenge Big Brother.

The Adventures of Huckleberry Finn
Brainstem Medulla Reticular Formation Amygdala Nucleus Accumbens Hippocampus Frontal Lobe / Prefrontal Cortex

Twain's frequent use of hyperbole often utilizes Huck's brainstem and medulla. Thinking he is alone on Jackson Island, he hears a sound:

"My heart jumped up amongst my lungs...But my breath come so hard I couldn't hear nothing else."

Huck's inability to lie to women may result from an overactive reticular formation. Unable to resist Mary Jane's beauty, he finally exposes the truth about the King and Duke: *"In my opinion she had more sand in her than any girl I ever see...And when it comes to beauty-- and goodness too--she lays over them all."* Perhaps the unspoken promise to his nucleus accumbens drives him to her allegiance.

Animal Farm
Frontal Lobe / Prefrontal Cortex

Snowball and Napoleon both distinguish themselves from the other animals with their intellect. Snowball's teaching the other animals to read and write and Napoleon's nefarious plotting to exploit his fellow animals are both results of their frontal lobe--specifically the prefrontal cortex. This is a good example of how frontal lobe activity can be employed in the services of good or evil.

The frontal lobe would be a good vantage point to compare and contrast Snowball and Napoleon.

The Awakening
Reticular Formation Nucleus Accumbens Frontal Lobe / Prefrontal Cortex
Edna Pontellier's attraction to Robert likely sets off her reticular formation. Every meeting with him rewards her overactive nucleus accumbens. However, her prefrontal cortex weighs the pros and cons of her emotional affair with Robert and decides that oblivion is preferable to self-betrayal.

"Bartleby the Scrivener"
Frontal Lobe / Prefrontal Cortex
Most bosses would quickly fire Bartleby for his unyielding insubordination. However, the narrator engages his frontal lobe and prefrontal cortex to regulate his anger and responds instead with sympathy. This impressive display of impulse control is a clear example of executive functioning of the brain.

Beowulf
Brainstem Medulla Amygdala Nucleus Accumbens
Beowulf's nucleus accumbens answers Hrothgar's call for a hero, with promise that his name will be memorialized for the vanquishing of Grendel. The flesh-eating monster strikes terror in the brainstem, medulla, and amygdala of all mortals--save for Beowulf alone. His absence of fear could indicate an underdeveloped amygdala.

Billy Budd
Amygdala Cerebellum
When Claggart falsely charges the innocent Billy Budd with insubordination, the "handsome sailor" is tongue-tied. However, his fists work just fine, as he strikes a deadly blow to Claggart: "The next instant, quick as the flame from a discharged cannon at night, his right arm shot out, and Claggart dropped to the deck. Whether intentionally or but owing to the young athlete's superior height, the blow had taken effect fully upon the forehead, so shapely and intellectual-looking a feature in the Master-at-arms; so that the body fell over lengthwise, like a heavy plank tilted from erectness. A gasp or two, and he lay motionless." In this momentary lack of self-control and instinctual self-preservation, Billy's amygdala and cerebellum cause him to quickly lash out and kill the insidious Claggart.

Brave New World

Reticular Formation Amygdala Nucleus Accumbens Frontal Lobe /Prefrontal Cortex

Soma's effect is to render the prefrontal cortex useless in its responsibility for cerebral thought and emotion regulation. Freed from thinking, its adherents are free to follow their reticular formation with the promise of inconsequential, free sex. The nucleus accumbens is addressed in the mindless refrain: "Orgy, porgy, Ford and fun, Kiss the girls and make them One. Boys at one with girls at peace. Orgy-porgy gives release." However, intentional blunting of the frontal lobe does not not work for John, who sadly cannot live in a world led by its collective reticular formation.

Candide

Reticular Formation Nucleus Accumbens Hippocampus Frontal Lobe / Prefrontal Cortex

Having once tasted Cunegonde's beauty, Candide's hippocampus cannot release the memory of their embrace. With his nucleus accumbens promising

117

carnal pleasure, he chases Cunegonde across the world.

Many, many tragedies later, having witnessed the full spectrum of human suffering, Candide employs frontal lobe thinking to reject Martin's view that "man was born to live either in the convulsions of misery, or in the lethargy of boredom." Likewise, his prefrontal cortex ultimately rejects the Panglossian platitude that we live in the "best of all possible worlds." Weighing his experiences, Candide's PFC finally accepts that "we must cultivate our garden" and reject philosophical pursuits.

The Catcher in the Rye

Frontal Lobe
Limbic System

Holden Caulfield describes an encounter with Sunny, the young prostitute:
"[S]he stood up and pulled her dress over her head. I certainly felt peculiar when she did that. I mean she did it so sudden and all. I know you're supposed to feel pretty sexy when somebody gets up and pulls their dress over their head, but I didn't. Sexy was about the last thing I was feeling. I felt much more depressed than sexy."
Rather than accept her carnal offerings, Holden's frontal lobe leads him to try to "...keep the old conversation going. She was a lousy conversationalist." In this attempt, Holden's depressed limbic system blunts his sexual desires while simultaneously driving him to connect socially with another human being.

The Crucible

Reticular Formation
Amygdala
Nucleus Accumbens
Hippocampus
Frontal Lobe / Prefrontal Cortex

When Abigail Williams first lays eyes on John Proctor in Act I, she "has stood as though on tiptoe, absorbing his presence, wide-eyed..." with an engaged reticular formation. Both she and John must regulate their nucleus accumbens, since each one's hippocampus cannot forget their infamous affair: "I know how you clutched my back behind your house and sweated like a stallion..." she cries with desire and promise. However, John alone employs his frontal lobe to resist her advances with his proclamation: "But I will cut off my hand before I'll ever reach for you again. Wipe it out of mind. We never touched, Abby." With this new fear of abandonment, Abigail finds new resolve to launch a wave of witchcraft accusations, culminating with the death of her former lover.

"The Fall of the House of Usher"

Amygdala
Frontal Lobe / Prefrontal Cortex

Poor Roderick Usher is tormented by numerous toxic, self-defeating beliefs. Among these are a "morbid acuteness of the senses"..."the opinion, in its general form, of the sentience of all living things" (including his house), and the resignation that "I must abandon life and reason together, in the struggle with the grim phantasm, FEAR." With this man a slave to his amygdala, his frontal lobe has no chance to save him, leaving the narrator to declare "To an anomalous species of terror I found him a bounden slave."

Fahrenheit 451

Frontal Lobe / Prefrontal Cortex
Hippocampus

With society in shambles, Granger introduces Montag to the network of people committed to memorizing the great works of literature: "We read the books and burnt them, afraid they'd be found. Micro-filming didn't pay off; we were always travelling, we didn't want to bury the film and come back later. Always the chance of discovery. Better to keep it in the old heads, where no one can see it or suspect it. We are all bits and pieces of history and literature and international law, Byron, Tom Paine, Machiavelli, or Christ, it's here." This incredible feat of memorization would require an impressive prefrontal cortex for organization and planning while relying upon a powerful hippocampus to help save the memories.

Frankenstein
Amygdala Frontal Lobe / Prefrontal Cortex
At the monster's "birth," the creature "muttered inarticulate sounds" with "one hand...stretched out" for his creator. Sadly, Victor's amygdala causes him to flee in terror: "I remained during the rest of the night, walking up and down in the greatest agitation, listening attentively, catching and fearing each sound as if it were to announce the approach of the demoniacal corpse to which I had so miserably given life." In a sad and ironic twist, Victor's prefrontal cortex managed the Herculean task of planning and executing the task of raising the dead back to life--but utterly failed to recognize the need of the newborn to be held. Had Victor's frontal lobe-- and not his amygdala--been utilized in this critical birth moment, multiple murders could have been avoided in the monster's quest for vengeance.

The Glass Menagerie
Reticular Formation Amygdala Nucleus Accumbens Hippocampus
Laura's reticular formation is evident when Jim walks into

the living room where she hides in terror and desire. Her hippocampus has helped her remember every detail of Jim's storied high school career. In turn, Jim's nucleus accumbens is seduced to validate her with a kiss. Later, Tom's amygdala is kicked into high gear when his mother Laura accuses him of setting up Laura with an engaged man. In a fit of fury, Tom's amygdala forces him to desert his family and continue the legacy of his absent father.

The Grapes of Wrath

Hippocampus
Frontal Lobe / Prefrontal Cortex

In a powerful scene that sears an image into the hippocampus, Uncle John chooses not to bury Rose of Sharon's stillborn baby. Instead, he places the baby corpse in a box and lets it float down river.
"Go down an' tell 'em. Go down in the street an' rot an' tell 'em that way. That's the way you can talk."
This serves as the baby's eulogy and Steinbeck's hope that this explicit memory will be imprinted upon the reader as well as the fictional world of the Joads. When Rose of Sharon saves the dying old man with the milk from her breast, "She looked up and across the barn, and her lips came together and smiled mysteriously." Here, her frontal lobe processes this moment reflectively as she realizes her life can still be suffused with meaning.

Great Expectations

Nucleus Accumbens
Reticular Formation
Prefrontal Cortex

The irresistible Estella plays to Pip's nucleus accumbens when she offers him an enticing kiss: "Instead of going straight to the gate, too, she stepped back into the passage, and beckoned me. "Come here! You may kiss me, if you like." I kissed her cheek as she turned it to me. I think I would have gone through a great deal to kiss her cheek." Like every femme fatale, Estella lights up every man's reticular formation with her beauty and empty flirtation. Pip doesn't stand a chance with his prefrontal cortex still under construction due to his tender age.

The Great Gatsby

Reticular Formation
Amygdala
Nucleus Accumbens
Hippocampus
Frontal Lobe / Prefrontal Cortex

Daisy's voice is the kind "...that the ear follows up and down as if each speech is an arrangement of notes that will never be played again"--tickling the reticular formation of every man who listens--especially Jay Gatsby. When Gatsby manages to kiss Daisy, "[a]t his lips touch she blossomed for him like a flower and the incarnation was complete." Here, the circuits in his limbic system are overwhelmed with desire as his nucleus accumbens activates with hope that this moment will springboard him into personal and social transformation. With this memory, forever imprinted on Gatsby's hippocampus, he utilizes his prefrontal cortex to navigate the underground dangers of the bootlegging industry to amass a fortune in his effort to secure Daisy's heart. Tragically, George Wilson's distraught amygdala has the final word as he shoots Gatsby in his swimming pool, and "the holocaust was complete."

Hamlet

Cerebellum
Amygdala
Nucleus Accumbens
Hippocampus
Frontal Lobe / Prefrontal Cortex

"Something is rotten in the state of Denmark." Indeed. But this enduring line is preceded by Hamlet's heightened nucleus accumbens. Seeing the ghost beckon him, Hamlet is tempted to follow. His friends, however, are worried about his safety and caution him to stay. Hamlet's nucleus accumbens responds accordingly:
"[U]nhand me gentlemen;--[breaking from them].
By heaven, I'll make a ghost of him that lets
me:--I say away..."
When Claudius later sees his crime reflected in The Mousetrap, his hippocampus lights up with the memory of his guilt:
O, my offense is rank, it smells to heaven;
It hath the primal eldest curse upon't,

A brother's murder!--Pray can I not..."
With secured knowledge of Claudius' guilt,
Hamlet is ready to run a sword through his chest.
However, his prefrontal cortex stays his sword
with this rationalization:
Now might I do it, pat, now he is praying;
And now I'll do't; and so he goes to heaven:
And so am I reveng'd? That would be scann'd:
A villain kills my father; and for that,
I, his sole son, do this same villain send
To heaven..."

***

If Laertes' cerebellum had not failed him, he may have
been the victor in his duel with Hamlet. Instead, he
stumbles, drops his poisonous sword, and inadvertently
switches "the treacherous instrument" with the hapless
prince. This end result is Laertes being "envenom'd" by
his own "foul practice." After Laertes' admission of guilt:
"the king, the king's to blame..." Hamlet and Claudius
both share inflamed amygdalas:

King: O, yet defend me friends, I am but hurt.
Hamlet: Here, thou incestuous, murd'rous,
damned Dane,
Drink off this potion:--Is the union here? Follow
my mother."

The Kite Runner
Brainstem Amygdala Hippocampus Frontal Lobe / Prefrontal Cortex

125

When Amir witnesses Hassan's rape by Assef, Amir's amygdala and brainstem freeze him in place, rendering him incapable of rescuing his dear friend: "I opened my mouth, almost said something. Almost. The rest of my life might have turned out differently if I had. But I didn't. I just watched. Paralyzed."

Forever imprinted onto Amir's hippocampus, he pronounces his fate: "My hands are stained with Hassan's blood." In adulthood, Amir attempts frontal lobe atonement by adopting Hassan's son Sohrab: "I pray God doesn't let them get stained with the blood of his boy too."

Lord of the Flies
Cerebellum Amygdala Frontal Lobe / Prefrontal Cortex
When the boys find themselves stranded on a deserted island with no adult help or supervision, two leaders emerge: Ralph and Jack. Each one represents different ideas of leadership, and each one easily represents the age-old power struggle between the fear-based amygdala and the rationalizing, thoughtful frontal lobe.With tribalism an amygdala behavior, Jack encapsulates this well in his fear-mongering call to followers: "Who'll join my tribe?"..."Kill the beast! Cut his throat! Spill his blood." In contrast, the ever rational Ralph clearly chooses frontal lobe leadership. Together with the PFC-dominated Piggy, they advocate fairness and democracy:" [W]hat intelligence had been shown was traceable to Piggy...But there was a stillness about

Ralph as he sat that marked him out: there was his size, and attractive appearance; and most obscurely, yet most powerfully, there was the conch. The being that had blown that...was set apart." Ralph's control over the conch demonstrates frontal lobe dominance over emotion and instinct.

Macbeth
Brainstem Medulla Amygdala Nucleus Accumbens
Hearing the prophecy "...none of woman born shall harm Macbeth," the Scottish king believes himself invincible. This overconfidence leads him to challenge Macduff, who informs him "...Macduff was from his mother's womb untimely ripped." Macbeth's amygdala is undoubtedly triggered with fear upon hearing this news and sends signals of retreat: "Accursed be that tongue that tells me so, For it hath cowed my better part of man! I'll not fight with thee." Yet Macbeth's frontal lobe rethinks his legacy. Though his brainstem and medulla may engage him in fight-or-flight behavior, he answers the call with his prefrontal cortex declaration: "Yet I will try the last. Before my body I throw my warlike shield. Lay on, Macduff, And damned be him that first cries 'Hold! Enough!'"

A Midsummer Night's Dream

Reticular Formation
Nucleus Accumbens

When Oberon sprinkles the magic potion on Titania's eyelids as she sleeps, it arouses her reticular formation upon waking: "In thy eye that shall appear When thou wak'st, it is thy dear." The potion creates further mischief as Lysander's nucleus accumbens drives him to pursue Helena, while Demetrius falls victim to his own nucleus accumbens--only satisfied in the presence of Hermia.

Moby-Dick

Hippocampus

Had Captain Ahab lived today, he probably would be diagnosed with PTSD after losing his leg to the White Whale. This traumatic moment was forever stamped upon his hippocampus, which absolutely cannot let him forget the past. This same hippocampus is a key player in his monomania: "I am madness maddened! That wild madness that's only calm to comprehend itself! ...Aye! I lost this leg. I now prophecy that I will dismember my dismemberer."

Night

Brainstem
Medulla
Reticular Formation
Cerebellum
Amygdala
Nucleus Accumbens

One of the most disturbing scenes in Night (...and there are many) depicts an old, starving man being strangled by his own son for bread. "Meir, Meir, my boy! Don't you recognize me? I'm your father...you're hurting me...you're killing your father! I've got some bread...for you too...for you too..." Is this a sociopathic moment for young Meir-- brought forth by his own starvation, abuse, and suffering by his Nazi captors? Though we know little about his personality before this moment, his horrific behavior can be partially attributed to the limbic players of his brainstem, medulla, nucleus accumbens, and--above all-- his amygdala. All of these brain structures work together, override any PFC regulation, and ensure his survival. However, his survival is short-lived, as his karmic debt is instantly paid: "He was not able to get very far. Two men had seen and hurled themselves upon him. Others joined in. When they withdrew, next to me were two corpses, side by side, the father and the Son." Was this mob justice? Were the onlookers observing through the lens of their frontal lobes? Did they decide in that instant that patricide must be unequivocally punished? Possibly. More likely they were motivated by their own limbic systems-- with the nucleus accumbens and amygdala leading the charge with the battle cry of hunger: "Get bread!"

Of Mice and Men

Cerebellum
Nucleus Accumbens
Reticular formation
Amygdala
Hippocampus
Frontal Lobe / Prefrontal Cortex

Though Lennie has been clearly instructed to avoid conversation with Curley's wife, she has other plans:

"Why can't I talk to you? I never get to talk to nobody. I get awful lonely." Lennie said, "Well, I ain't supposed to talk to you or nothing."

"I get lonely," she said. "You can talk to people, but I can't talk to nobody but Curley. Else he gets mad. How'd you like not to talk to anybody?"

Lennie said, "Well, I ain't supposed to. George's scared I'll get in trouble."

Here, the reader can see Lennie's frontal lobe at work, as his nucleus accumbens is promised the reward of female flirtation, but his prefrontal cortex tries to keep such behavior at bay. However, Curley's wife is relentless as she dangles her hair in front of his reticular formation:

"When I'm doin' my hair sometimes I jus' set an' stroke it 'cause it's so soft."

With Lennie's PFC losing the battle, his amygdala kicks into high gear for his self-preservation:

"Don't you go yellin'," he said, and he shook her; and her body flopped like a fish. And then she was still, for Lennie had broken her neck.

With his cerebellum losing control of the strength and movement of his hands, Lennie must flee for his life. In one of literature's most anguishing conclusions, George's PFC must weigh the options of administering Lennie a quick, merciful death or surrendering him to the prolonged, torturous death by Curley's mob. Before pulling the trigger to end Lennie's life, George appeals to Lennie's dependable hippocampus to pull a pleasant memory out of storage: Lennie said, "Tell how it's gonna be....We gonna get a little place."

The Odyssey

Reticular formation
Nucleus Accumbens
Frontal Lobe / Prefrontal Cortex

Having been forewarned by the prophet Circe, Odysseus knows his frontal lobe is no match for the powers of the Sirens on his limbic system, particularly his aroused reticular formation. Therefore, he speaks pre-emptively to his men through his prefrontal cortex:

"Therefore you are to tie me up, tight as a splint, erect along the mast, lashed to the mast, and if I shout and beg to be untied, take more turns of the rope to muffle me."

However, "[t]he lovely voices in ardor appealing over the water made [him] crave to listen, and [he] tried to say 'Untie me!' to the crew, jerking [his] brows, but they bent steady to the oars."

Despite the efforts of his nucleus accumbens to thwart the restrains of his frontal lobe, Odysseus and his men survive thanks to his prefrontal thinking.

The Picture of Dorian Gray

Nucleus Accumbens
Prefrontal Cortex

Lord Henry Wotten, a deviant speaker of aphorisms, is a master at PFC-manipulation. His twist of words, no matter how logical and profound they may seem, are targeted towards the nucleus accumbens of the listener—most especially that of Dorian's.

"Beauty is a form of Genius--is higher, indeed, than Genius, as it needs no explanation....It has its divine right of sovereignty....People say sometimes that beauty is only superficial. That may be so. But at least it is not so superficial as Thought is."

Though Lord Henry uses his frontal lobe to deliver this obvious sophism, Dorian neglects to utilize his own. The net result is his inevitable downfall.

Pride and Prejudice

Nucleus Accumbens
Frontal Lobe / Prefrontal Cortex

Elizabeth Bennet's conflicted relationship with Mr. Darcy depicts the classic pull between the nucleus accumbens and the rational prefrontal cortex. Darcy's social status and considerable wealth clearly play on the reward circuit of Elizabeth's brain:

"...[T]he eye was instantly caught by Pemberley

House....It was a large, handsome, stone building...Elizabeth was delighted....at that moment, she felt that to be mistress of Pemberley might be something!"

However, her strained relationship with Darcy prevents the couple from engaging in sincere, authentic dialogue. The catalyst that changes this equation is Darcy's secret plot to save Lydia from public disgrace. Upon learning that Darcy actively took steps to protect her sister's reputation while seeking no reward or credit, Elizabeth's prefrontal cortex takes over:

"Elizabeth soon observed, and instantly understood it. Her power was sinking; everything must sink under such a proof of family weakness, such an assurance of the deepest disgrace. She could neither wonder nor condemn, but the belief of his self-conquest brought nothing consolatory to her bosom, afforded no palliation of her distress. It was, on the contrary, exactly calculated to make her understand her own wishes; and never had she so honestly felt she could have loved him, as now...."

This is the quintessential moment of character development--when a dynamic character utilizes her frontal lobe, processes new information, and exhibits growth.

A Raisin in the Sun
Amygdala Hippocampus Frontal Lobe / Prefrontal Cortex
When Walter Younger is conned out of his family's

fortune by Willy Harris, his amygdala shifts him into survival mode. In his desperation, he plans to accept Lindner's offer to buy out his family's house contract in an all-white neighborhood. In the language of his amygdala, Walter tells Mama:

"I'm going to look that son-of-a-bitch in the eyes and say...'All right, Mr. Lindner...that's your neighborhood out there! You got the right to keep it like you want! You got the right to have it like you want! Just write the check and--the house is yours...And you--you people just put the money in my hand and you won't have to live next this bunch of stinking...."

At a later moment, when Walter must sign Lindner's offer, his prefrontal cortex takes the controls:

"Travis, come here...This is my son, and he makes the sixth generation our family in this country. And we have all thought about your offer...And we have decided to move into our house because my father-- my father--he earned it for us brick by brick."

Mama declares that Walter "...finally come into his manhood today, didn't he? Kind of like a rainbow after the rain..."

This is an apt description of the triumph of Walter's frontal lobe over his amygdala and limbic system. As the family packs up and leaves their apartment one final time before moving to their new house, Mama's hippocampus causes her to look "...around at all the walls and ceilings, and suddenly, despite herself, while the children call below, a great heaving thing rises in her and she puts her fist to her mouth to stifle it...."

No doubt, she vividly recalls countless memories of her family in the tiny apartment over the decades. Her limbic system, led by her hippocampus, floods her with emotional memories one last time. But in her dignity, she, "...pulls her coat about her, pats her hat and goes out."

The Red Badge of Courage

Brainstem
Medulla
Cerebellum
Amygdala
Nucleus Accumbens
Hippocampus
Frontal Lobe / Prefrontal Cortex

As the bullets and mortar shells begin to fly, Henry Fleming runs for his life. His worst fear--flight over fight in battle--has materialized. His brainstem and medulla seize control, dispelling any semblance of heroics:

"He ran like a rabbit.... He yelled then with a fright and swung about. For a moment, with great clamour, he was like a proverbial chicken. He lost the direction of safety. Destruction threatened him from all points."

His cerebellum fails him as he loses direction and balance, "...speeding towards the rear in great leaps." With his amygdala tightening its grip on his will, Henry survives--albeit only physically. However, his journey is far from over. With many emerging battles, the Civil War offers multiple opportunities for redemption. Henry later distinguishes himself in battle and indeed becomes the flag bearer for his regiment:

"The youth walked stolidly into the midst of the mob, and with his flag in his hands took a stand." With this memory logged into his hippocampus, Henry's prefrontal cortex can now reflect on his fears, his courage, and his growth:

"Yet, the youth smiled, for he saw that the world was a world for him.... He had rid himself of the red sickness of battle. The sultry nightmare was in the past. He had been an animal blistered and sweating in the heat and pain of war. He turned now with a lover's thirst to images of tranquil skies, fresh meadows, cool brooks--an existence of soft and eternal peace."

No longer "the youth," Henry is now a man. A man with a fully functioning frontal lobe that rules over his amygdala.

Romeo and Juliet

Reticular Formation
Nucleus Accumbens
Frontal Lobe
Hippocampus
Prefrontal Cortex
Limbic System

What is the real tragedy of literature's famous star-crossed lovers? Though many may cite the folly of the Capulet/Montague feud, neuroscience may reveal one more localized to the adolescent brain. The culprit reveals itself the moment Romeo first spies Juliet:

"Oh, she doth teach the torches to burn bright!
It seems she hangs upon the cheek of night
Like a rich jewel in an Ethiope's ear, Beauty too rich
for use, for earth too dear. So shows a snowy dove

trooping with crows. As yonder lady o'er her fellows shows. The measure done, I'll watch her place of stand, And, touching hers, make blessed my rude hand. Did my heart love till now? Forswear it, sight! For I ne'er saw true beauty till this night."

In this critical moment, Romeo's reticular formation is in red alert, with his nucleus accumbens throbbing in the hopes of winning this paragon of perfected beauty. His frontal lobe, however, is missing in action. Why else would he claim he had never loved before? And never seen beauty before? Does the name Rosaline mean nothing? Evidently, her memory was never saved in his hippocampus. With even more disregard, Juliet completely ignores her prefrontal cortex and follows a momentary impulse:

"Then I'll be brief. O happy dagger,
[Taking Romeo's dagger]
This is my sheath;
[Stabs herself]
There rust, and let me die."

The word "brief" captures the tragedy. The activity of her limbic system is brief--caught in a single moment of time. Her ignoring her frontal lobe is likewise brief. But this brevity is enough to end her life--and ironically lasts an eternity.

Thus, the tragedy of Romeo and Juliet is one applicable to all humanity...ignore our frontal lobe at our peril.

The Scarlet Letter

Amygdala
Frontal Lobe / Prefrontal Cortex
Nucleus Accumbens

Roger Chillingworth is a unique villain with the capacity to utilize the higher functioning abilities of his frontal lobe to plot and perpetrate evil. Discovering an adulterous wife would fire up the amygdala of the average man, responding with a fiery limbic system thirsting for revenge. But Chillingworth's prefrontal cortex reigns in his impulses and patiently plants seeds of vengeance towards Dimmesdale.

The net effect? Cumulative psychological and physical duress on the unsuspecting minister. While Dimmesdale naps innocently in his study, Chillingworth "...thrust aside the vestment, that, hitherto, had always covered it even from the professional eye." Seeing an apparent "A" upon Dimmesdale's chest, Chillingworth dances a jig in the same manner that "...Satan comports himself when a precious human soul is lost to heaven and won into his kingdom."

In this disturbing moment, Chillingworth's nucleus accumbens and his prefrontal cortex rejoice together as passion and planning become one. Though a villain, his cerebral control is indeed impressive.

Siddhartha
Reticular Formation Nucleus Accumbens Frontal Lobe / Prefrontal Cortex
As a young man seeking enlightenment, Siddhartha carefully guards his chastity. When seduced by a young, beautiful woman, "Siddhartha also felt a longing and the stir of sex in him; but as he had never yet touched a woman, he hesitated a moment...." Ah, the quintessential moment when the reticular formation lights up with arousal as the frontal lobe tries to quell its activity! "At that moment he heard his inward voice and the voice said 'No!'..Gently he stroked her cheek and quickly disappeared..." as his prefrontal cortex celebrates its temporary victory. The celebration ends, of course, when he meets Kamala.

"The Tell-Tale Heart"
Brainstem Medulla Reticular Formation Nucleus Accumbens Frontal Lobe / Prefrontal Cortex
After the murder and dismemberment of his landlord, the narrator painfully endures the chatter of police as they "...sat talking with me in a friendly way." At that moment, his brainstem and

medulla take over. His heartbeat quickens, and his breathing becomes shallow as his sympathetic nervous system kicks into high gear:

"...I must have become quite white. I talked still faster and louder. And the sound, too, became louder. It was a quick, low, soft sound, like the sound of a clock heard through a wall, a sound I knew well. Louder it became, and louder."

The heartbeat, unquestionably loud, is more likely his own as it pumps blood to his muscles in full fight-or-flight response.

Their Eyes Were Watching God

Reticular Formation
Nucleus Accumbens
Frontal Lobe / Prefrontal Cortex

Every man who sets eyes on Janie feels the activation of his reticular formation:

"The men noticed her firm buttocks like she had grape fruits in her hip pockets; the great rope of black hair swinging to her waist and unraveling in the wind like a plume; then her pugnacious breasts trying to bore holes in her shirt. They, the men were saving with the mind what they lost with the eye."

But only Tea Cake rises above his reticular formation. He is the only one to engage her via his frontal lobe. Recognizing her independence, Tea Cake wins her heart with a game of checkers:

"He set it up and began to show her and she found

herself glowing inside. Somebody wanted her to play. Somebody thought it natural for her to play."

Tea Cake uses not only his frontal lobe, but asks Janie to use her prefrontal cortex to beat him in checkers. For his efforts, his nucleus accumbens is abundantly rewarded:

"They wrestled on until they were doped with their own fumes and emanations; till their clothes
had been torn off...."

The Things They Carried

Amygdala
Frontal Lobe
Limbic System
Prefrontal Cortex
Hippocampus

The narrator, an American soldier in Vietnam, describes the experience of killing a man: "I had already thrown the grenade before telling myself to throw it."

In this moment, his amygdala, in survival mode, gives orders before the rational frontal lobe can react. "I was terrified," he says in the amygdala's language. "It was not a matter of live or die. There was no real peril."

"There was no sound at all--none that I can remember--" he recalls. This is likely the effect of his highly energized limbic system, so keenly terrified for his survival and overwhelmed with the stimuli of the environment. In later years, his prefrontal cortex reflects upon his lingering connection to the dead man, as he realizes that living and dead share an eerie, unshakeable connection:

"Even now I haven't finished sorting it out....I'll look up and see the young man coming out of the morning fog. I'll watch him walk toward me, his shoulders slightly stooped, his head cocked to the side...and suddenly smile...."

Touchingly, the memory of this young man has been forever imprinted upon his hippocampus, lest he forget.

CHAPTER EIGHT

PUTTING IT ALL TOGETHER

Congrats on getting this far! If your head hurts a little after all that psychological jargon, let's put it all in a "to-go" container:

Chapter	Takeaway
1	Identify the tension of opposites. Every conflict will have these.
2a	Clearly identify which forces are being dramatized. This can be helpful in a thesis statement, topic sentence, or main idea. Questions to consider: Which force is obvious? Which force is implied? Which force is painful? Which one is linked to growth of the character?
2b	Examine the events before and after the forces. (A flowchart is a good idea.)
3	Explore the needs of your character. These could be physical, emotional, social, etc.
4	Examine the unconscious forces in your character's mind. Examples: id, ego, superego, childhood experiences, relationships with parents, sexual impulses, etc. This may also reveal unmet needs.

5	Consider character archetypes. If your character fits one, look for opposing forces around this archetype. These forces can be positive, negative, or both.
6	Explore mental disorders. If you character potentially has one (e.g., anxiety or depression disorders), investigate what led to it, and what happens as a result of it. Take a look at the pain that caused it, and the pain that follows it.
7	Which parts of the brain could be used to explain your character's behavior? If she struggles with **reason vs. emotion** (probably the most common conflict), consider her **frontal lobe and limbic system**.

Notice that much of this intellectual pursuit is about opposing forces. It's what started our journey. And it's what we're left with at the end of the day.

A Final Note

This is by no means a list of all things psychological in the world of literature, but it's enough to get you started using psychology to analyze more deeply. I hope literature can at least stimulate your interest to learn more about psychology-- and vice versa.

There seems to be an endless battle between the humanities and the sciences. It's time to smoke the peace pipe! And maybe we can do that by reading **Literature through Psychology!**

APPENDIX A: SAMPLE STUDENT ESSAYS

Student Essay #1

Dr. White

AP Literature and Composition

8 March 2019

Fractured and Incomplete

Plato once said that "according to Greek mythology,

humans were originally created with four arms, four legs and a head

with two faces. Fearing their power, Zeus split them into two

separate parts, condemning them to spend their lives in search of

their other halves" (Plato 13). At surface level, it seems that the

Greek myth that Plato recalls is an ode to the power of love and an

attestation to the existence of a soulmate. Yet, beneath that surface

is a darker truth: humans are all fractured and incomplete, fulfilled

only through a union with some other half. Like the humans in

Plato's Greek myth, the Monster in Mary Shelley's novel,

Frankenstein, is fractured and incomplete. He is mercilessly

abandoned by society and forced to navigate the world and his own

needs utterly alone. Although the Monster is the most apparent

example of an incomplete human with a plethora of unfulfilled

needs, he is not the only example that Shelley provides. In fact,

nearly all of the principal characters in *Frankenstein*—the Monster,

147

Victor, Henry, and Elizabeth—are in some way, incomplete. It is through their collective journeys to their other halves that Shelley unearths the darker side of the human condition, and more specifically, the dogged pursuit of man's universal needs.

The Monster and his creator, Victor Frankenstein, are continually portrayed in the novel as two opposing forces at odds with one another; however, both characters are intrinsically linked and possess many fundamental similarities. Their relationship is characterized by the magnitude of their loathing for one another and for themselves. The Monster aptly reminds Frankenstein of this, telling him that "You hate me, but your abhorrence cannot equal that with which I regard myself" (Shelley 167). This deep hatred that they both possess is simply a more bearable manifestation of all of the pain that they have incurred throughout their lives. Psychologist Bernard Golden comments on this relationship between pain and hatred, claiming that individuals "consumed by hate may believe that the only way to regain some sense of power over his or her pain is to preemptively strike out at others. In this context, each moment of hate is a temporary reprieve from inner suffering" (Abrams 3). This phenomenon is apparent in how Frankenstein vengefully hunts down the monster in order to evade the pain of losing Elizabeth. The Monster's devolution from social outcast to sociopathic murderer exemplifies this as well, as it is through terrorizing others that the Monster attempts to overcome the pain of rejection.

On the other side of the spectrum are characters like Henry Clerval and Elizabeth. Although they seem like the most developed, well-rounded characters in the novel, they are not without faults. Primarily, both characters are flawed in that they are overly dependent upon Victor, and almost seem to solely exist to serve him. Their unwavering bond with Victor gives Shelley numerous opportunities to juxtapose their lighthearted demeanor and love of nature with the darkness of Victor's deeds and tribulations. While Victor sees himself as "a shattered wreck—the shadow of a human being" (Shelley 139) Henry is described in sweet and innocent terms, as enjoying "happiness seldom tasted by man" (Shelley 120). The contrast between these characters offers commentary on the importance of learning to live in the moment, amid all that one needs, rather than to live in the future, chasing after distant desires. Their deep relationship suggests that both sides of humanity, the light and the dark, can only survive together. Thus, it is only in the absence of Henry and Elizabeth that Victor fully devolves into that vengeful and truly broken "shadow of a human being" (Shelley 139).

Perhaps Mary Shelley chose to feature so many broken characters in her novel because they all represented different parts of a dysfunctional whole. Sigmund Freud's theory of a tripartite human psyche—the Id, Ego, and Superego—can provide a framework to analyze the connections between the characters. The Monster, like the id, is "primitive and instinctual" and driven by aggressive drives (McLeod 1). The more elevated Henry and Elizabeth function as the superego, while Victor is the core of the novel, the ego, that "mediates between the desires of the id and the superego," (McLeod 1) or in this case the desires of innocence or living in the moment and vengefulness. Ultimately, Mary Shelley's *Frankenstein* is a depiction of the failure and fission of the human psyche in obtaining its needs.

On the outskirts of the novel is one more last, vital character—Robert Walton. Despite his many parallels to the journey of Victor Frankenstein, he defies Victor in many ways, and thus offers the audience a sense of hope in the possibility of growth and positive change. Victor's story teaches Walton that "if we are lost, my mad schemes are the cause" (Shelley 160). His choice to give in to the demands of his crew exemplifies his acceptance of that lesson. Walton redefines what it means to be brave, as he shows strength in making the seemingly cowardly decision to give up. In a way, Walton defies the undercurrent of the novel as a whole—he chooses to not search for that other half, whether it be scientific discovery, vengeance, or even a soulmate. In giving up what he wants, Walton discovers what he needs.

Works Cited

Abrams, Allison. "The Psychology of Hate." *Psychology Today*, Sussex Publishers, 9 Mar. 2017, www.psychologytoday.com/us/blog/nurturing-self-compassion/201703/the-psychology-hate.

McLeod, Saul. "Id, Ego and Superego." *Simply Psychology*, Simply Psychology, 5 Feb. 2017, www.simplypsychology.org/psyche.html.

Plato. "The Symposium." Translated by Benjamin Jowett, *The Internet Classics Archive | On Airs, Waters, and Places by Hippocrates*, MIT, classics.mit.edu/Plato/symposium.html.

Shelley, Mary. *Frankenstein*. Digireads.com, 2015.

Student Essay #2

Dr. Patrick White

AP English Literature and Composition

12 March 2019

Frankenstein Research Paper

A large portion of Mary Shelley's famous novel

Frankenstein is dedicated to an emotional detailing of the monster's

history, as told by the monster himself. Within these passages

readers may find distinct parallels between the monster's struggle

for survival and what humans have defined as basic needs--items

such as food, water, and shelter for the physical realm, but also

progression, acceptance, and self-esteem for the internal self.

Psychologists have recently theorized that some of these

metaphysical needs are universal amongst every living human.

Although Shelley may not have considered the transferability of the

lessons her monster is forced to learn over the course of his life,

they nevertheless are applicable to the emotional and mental

necessities of all of mankind.

According to the self-determination theory of

psychological motivation, humans at their best are "curious, vital,

and self-motivated, …striving to learn, …[mastering] new skills,"

(Ryan and Deci), and thus any needs of an individual attempt to meet these performance characteristics. Frankenstein's monster possesses such characteristics in his early life, in which he "thrust [his] hand into the live embers, but quickly drew it out again with a cry of pain," (Shelley 103) in a curiosity-driven attempt to understand fire, and later "discovered the names... [and] learned and applied the words...," (Shelley 111) when striving to comprehend language. Thus, one can see that the monster has at the very least similar intrinsic characteristics for motivation as humans; therefore his subsequent needs fittingly reflect those of man.

The self-determination theory (SDT) notes three major necessities for mental and emotional satisfaction and growth: "competence, relatedness, and autonomy," (Ryan and Deci). The monster exemplifies competence and autonomy with no issues; he "improved rapidly in the knowledge of language, so that in two months [he] began to comprehend most of the words uttered..." (Shelley 117), proving his competence, and his creator left him with the fullest and most extreme form of autonomy, that which is given by complete solitude. Unfortunately, this solitude proves to be the monster's greatest difficulty, as it hinders him in meeting the third need: relatedness and connection to others. The relatedness need is so critical to emotional well-being that some have expanded it into a fuller, more inclusive term meaning an individual's need "to be known and valued by him/herself and important others," (Henriques). However, the monster continuously fails to receive the love and ability to share experiences and thoughts that are associated with this need, despite some contending it as "the single most important variable in human development," (Henriques).

Frankenstein's monster's incompletion of the relatedness need has dire consequences on his psyche, most of which are expressed through his actions and verbal mirroring of thoughts. Such consequences are predicted by the SDT, which warns that "the darker side of human behavior and experience is understood in terms of basic needs having been thwarted," (Culham). The monster "longed to join [his human protectors]," and desired to "win first their favour, and afterwards their love," (Shelley 109-114), but he matches this prognosticated effect on man's emotional and mental growth when these hopes are ruined. Although he works towards meeting the relatedness and love need, he is not offered "ongoing nutriments and support from the social environment," (Culham), causing "all within [him] to turn to gall and bitterness," (Shelley 139). The internal universal human needs, when not met, appear to have drastic effects on worldviews and personality, and perhaps through her novel Shelley unintentionally warns mankind of creating a monster such as Frankenstein's. By considering the necessities of the mind and emotions as proven by modern psychology, society may better fend off belittlement, authoritarianism, and solitude that thwarts competence, autonomy, and relatedness. Hopefully, through considering the monster's plight and pitiful outcome, humans may reach a better communal understanding of themselves and each other.

Works Cited

Culham, Brett. "The Emotional Needs Scale." *Human Givens Institute*, 24 Jan. 2018, www.hgi.org.uk/resources/delve-our-extensive-library/resources-and-techniques/emotional-needs-scale.

Henriques, Gregg. "The Core Need." *Psychology Today*, Sussex Publishers, 25 June 2014, www.psychologytoday.com/us/blog/theory-knowledge/201406/the-core-need.

Ryan, Richard M, and Edward L Deci. *Self-Determination Theory and the Facilitation of Intrinsic Motivation, Social Development, and Well-Being*. University of Rochester, mofetinternational.macam.ac.il/jtec/Documents/Self-Determination%20Theory%20and%20the%20Facilitatio n%20of%20Intrinsic%20Motivation,%20Social%20Dev elopment,%20and%20Well-Being.pdf.

Shelley, Mary Wollstonecraft., and Karen Karbiener. *Frankenstein*. Barnes & Noble, 2003.

Dr. White

AP Literature

11 March 2019

Birth

Bright lights. He was yanked from the warmth and security of his mother's womb to the cold and ruthless world. Hands scrambled for his body as he struggled to stretch his legs in the newfound space. All of a sudden, his only form of physiological needs was cut. He was now on his own at the vulnerability of human needs. "We are born weak, we need strength; helpless, we need aid; foolish, we need reason." - (Jean-Jacques Rousseau). In Mary Shelley's novel *Frankenstein*, the protagonist, Victor Frankenstein took life into his own hands and created a inhuman yet of flesh and blood being. Instead of a natural conceived birth, he was brought to life by a strike of lightning. According to American psychologist, Abraham Maslow, humans have a certain number of needs. He categorized them into a pyramid called Maslow's Hierarchy of Needs. The monster's survival needs were similar to that of a human's. The psychological needs required for everyone human begins at birth.

Once the monster is created, it "formed a more horrid contrast"(Shelley 55), Dr. Frankenstein is appalled by his creation, saying "the beauty of the dream vanished and breathless horror and disgust filled my heart"(Shelley 55), therefore abandoning it. Instead of receiving the love from his creator, he was left alone to fend for himself. The beginning of Maslow's Hierarchy of Needs are "physiological needs - these are biological requirements for human survival, e.g. air, food, drink"(Mcleod). He "gazed with a kind of wonder"(Shelley 102) and "felt light, and hunger, and thirst"(Shelley 102); the physiological needs.

With his physiological needs meet and continuing to "distinguish his sensations from each other"(Shelley 102), he ventured off into the woods until he stumbles upon a family of villagers. He hides outside the house and observes them until he feels safe in their security, despite their unawareness of his existence. Books *Paradise Lost* and *Plutarch's Lives* teach him to speak and read English, thus gaining security in himself. In fact, he feels secure to the point where he takes a step to talk to the blind man and "introduce himself into the cottage of his protectors"(Shelley 131), satisfying the safety need.

The urge for connection can been seen as far as the beginning with Adam and Eve. God created two, proving that humans are fragile and made to be connected. The monster's desire for connection is evident as he enters the house and speaks with the blind man. Connection begins to form until the young villager Felix returns "strikes him violently"(Shelley 134) until he leaves. The drive reduction theory states that "a physiological need creates an aroused tension state that motivates an organism to satisfy that need"(Myers). The monster coveted love, as he watched his creator prepare for a wedding. This need of love and belonging forces the monster to beg his creator to "create a female for me, with whom I can live in the interchange of those sympathies necessary for my being"(Shelley 144). In hope that with a female, the monster will disappear without trouble, Dr. Frankenstein "consents to his demand"(Shelley 147) of creation of a female. When all seems well, he destroys the female in the process, in fear of major destruction as a result. This angers the monster and he vows to "be with him on his wedding night"(Shelley 167). With vengeance in mind, the monster kills Victor's newly-wed wife, Elizabeth. Victor dies soon after, just as the monster approaches. Realizing, his quest was near complete, he goes off to "ascend my funeral pile triumphantly, and exult in the agony of the torturing flames"(Shelley 120), descending the hierarchy.

The monster never got the chance to reach self-esteem or actualization. His need for love and belongingness were not met, prohibiting him to climb higher up the pyramid. Once humans emerge for the womb, their needs must be met. The vulnerability of the human species is proven through their struggle to survive. "From birth, humans are weak and in need of aid and strength"("Jean-Jacques Rousseau Quotes."). Humans, with the fragility that comes with life, are helpless creatures, in desperate need of acceptance.

Works Cited

"Jean-Jacques Rousseau Quotes." *BrainyQuote*, Xplore,

www.brainyquote.com/quotes/jeanjacques_rousseau_

47554? src=t_birth.

Mcleod, Saul. "Maslow's Hierarchy of Needs." *Simply Psychology*,

Simply Psychology, 21 May 2018,

www.simplypsychology.org/maslow.html.

Myers, David G. *Psychology: David G. Myers*. 2nd ed., Worth,

2001.

Shelley, Mary Wollstonecraft., and Karen Karbiener.

Frankenstein. Barnes & Noble, 2003.

APPENDIX B: LITERARY WORKS

Titles

NOTES

Made in the USA
Coppell, TX
09 November 2019